S0-BZH-511

THE FORGOTTEN COMMANDMENT

THE FORGOTTEN COMMANDMENT

EXPERIENCE THE POWER OF
HONORING YOUR PARENTS

DENNIS
RAINEY
WITH DAVID BOEHI

FamilyLife Publishing®
Little Rock, Arkansas

THE FORGOTTEN COMMANDMENT: Experience the Power of Honoring Your Parents
FamilyLife Publishing®
5800 Ranch Drive
Little Rock, Arkansas 72223
1-800-FL-TODAY • FamilyLife.com

FLTI, d/b/a FamilyLife®, is a ministry of Campus Crusade for Christ International®.

Originally published as *The Tribute* © Dennis Rainey, 1994 and *The Tribute and The Promise* © Dennis Rainey, 1994

ISBN: 978-1-60200-677-5

Some names have been changed to protect identities.

Design: Faceout® Studio
Cover Image: Thinkstock

Printed in the United States of America

18 17 16 15 14 1 2 3 4 5

DEDICATION

To Mom and Dad,
You are worthy of honor.

CONTENTS

FOREWORD

Author's Note: This foreword was written by my dear friend and mentor, Bill Bright, when the first edition of this book was published as *The Tribute* in 1994. Bill Bright lived as a truly honorable man to the day of his home going in 2003.

My precious and saintly mother, and equally loved and deeply appreciated father, have been with our Lord for many years. They both died at the age of ninety-three.

From my earliest youth, I have loved, obeyed, and honored my parents. They were very special to me. As I recall our relationship through the years, thousands of fond and treasured thoughts flood my mind. Gratefully, I have never had any significant negative, unhappy encounters with my parents.

Without question, my love for and happy relationship with my father and mother have greatly influenced and enriched my relationship with God. Indeed, my view of God, my ability to love, trust, and obey Him, and my eagerness to surrender my life completely without reservation to the lordship of Christ can be attributed at least in part to my godly parents.

Our attitudes toward our parents truly influences our attitudes toward our God, our Lord and Savior Jesus Christ.

The relationship between a parent and a child is one of the most important in our lives, regardless of our age. That is why I have been disturbed by the growing trend of "blaming parents" in our present society. In an effort to understand their own emotional struggles, many adults unfairly condemn their parents rather than take biblical responsibility upon themselves.

I believe that following the command of Scripture to love God with all our heart, soul, and mind, the mandate to honor our father and mother may be the most important of the Ten Commandments. Throughout my life, I have had opportunity to counsel with many thousands of people and have found in the process that those who have unresolved anger and resentment toward their parents are incapable of loving and obeying God with utter abandonment.

In *The Tribute* [now *The Forgotten Commandment*], Dennis Rainey has found that, for many adults, honoring parents is one of the most important steps of faith they can take. You will read many stories of triumph, about people who have obeyed God in honoring their parents, who in many cases have been harmed or wronged by the very ones whom God has commanded us to honor. God's command is not only for the benefits and blessing of the parents but for the children as well, because unresolved anger and resentment toward parents robs the child of God's blessing.

If you are not satisfied with your relationship with your parents, this could be one of the most important books you will ever read. Honoring your parents and writing a tribute to them could revolutionize your life, your relationship with them, and your relationship with God.

—Bill Bright

ACKNOWLEDGMENTS

Writing a book is like planting and maintaining an orchard. It requires the time, attention, energy, and commitment of skilled men and women who want to see an end product that yields much fruit. *The Forgotten Commandment* is no different.

My friend and partner in ministry Dave Boehi deserves a medal for his tireless service and painstaking care in helping shape this manuscript. Dave, I deeply appreciate the work that you did on this book and all that you do at FamilyLife.

Tim Grissom has once again proven that a good friend with a sharp pen is a true asset. Thanks for making this a far more effective book. I appreciate you.

I am also grateful for the publishing team God has assembled here at FamilyLife, and especially those who headed the effort to get this book in the hands of the reader—Leslie Barner, Tanisha Johnson, Rob Tittle, Tracy Lane, and Lida Damien. Thank you for your hard work and faithfulness.

To my children and their spouses: Ashley, Michael, Ben, MK, Samuel, Stephanie, Rebecca, Jacob, Deborah, and Laura. Thank you for honoring your mom and me more than we deserve. Your lives are tributes to God!

Finally, and mostly, a giant thank you to Barbara, my partner, friend, and fellow warrior in life. I want you to know how much I appreciate you. Thanks for being a committed woman of God. You are the best!

INTRODUCTION

ARE YOU READY FOR AN INCREDIBLE JOURNEY?

We all long to be in a right relationship with our parents, but few of us realize that the key to this relationship can be found in one of the Ten Commandments: "Honor your father and your mother" (Exodus 20:12).

This command—full of hope and promise—may be one of the most profound in Scripture. Indeed, I believe there are unforeseen benefits linked to one's obedience to this command:

- Could it be that you will forge a deeper, more meaningful relationship with your parents by honoring them?
- Could it be that God will be honored and pleased when you honor your parents?
- Could it be that your parents are just as desperate as you are to receive approval and affirmation?
- Could it be that the quality of life you experience today is directly tied to your obedience to this command?
- Could it be that a part of your longing and quest to become an adult is connected with honoring your parents?
- Could it be that obeying this commandment is an important test of your relationship with God?

Since this book was first published in 1994, I've heard from hundreds of readers who have told me stories of how they have honored their parents. These stories have convinced me that wherever you are in your relationship with your parents—whether it is great, okay, strained, or estranged—there is hope and encouragement for you in these pages. And I can promise you one thing: If you are willing to take an honest look at your relationship with your parents and seek ways to honor them, working through this issue may be one of the most profound, incredible experiences of your life.

How do I know this? Because that's what adult children have been telling me for over two decades.

That's why I can promise you that this will be one of the most important journeys of your lifetime.

(1)

THE CONNECTION

How sharper than a serpent's tooth
it is to have a thankless child.
—William Shakespeare

The scene is forever etched in my mind. It was August of 1966, and I stood in the driveway of my home in Ozark, Missouri, leaning against my white Chevrolet Bel Air.

I was eighteen years old, and I was about to leave home.

Boxes and suitcases filled the trunk and the backseat. My spinning rod could be seen through the back window, bent and pressed to conform to the rear deck. In the house, my bedroom was abandoned and lonely, littered with reminders of the boy who had claimed that space as his own for eighteen years. In a few minutes I would drive off to my new home—a dorm room at Crowder Junior College in Neosho, Missouri.

There were Dad and Mom, about to face an empty nest. Mom seemed especially short that day standing next to Dad, his arm around her waist. I was about to leave home and change our relationship forever.

Looking back, I can see that I was "bushwhacked," as Dad would say, by the emotion of that moment. No one had warned me that leaving home would be so difficult. No one had told me that the metamorphosis of a boy becoming a man would begin in earnest when he left home and headed for college.

I felt an enormous sense of gratitude and appreciation for these two people.

I can imagine what Ward and Dalcie Rainey were feeling at that moment, because Barbara and I have now launched all six of our children. They were thinking about the little boy who used to build mountains and roads in the sandbox next to the driveway. The sight of my fishing pole no doubt sparked memories of Dad and me catching white bass in Swan Creek.

For the first time in my life, I felt an enormous sense of gratitude and appreciation for these two people who had given me so much of themselves and had fashioned my life.

As I looked them in the eyes the emotion rose suddenly in my throat. As I moved to embrace them I swallowed hard, fought off the tears, and said, "Mom, Dad, I love you."

It was the first time I remember saying those words.

In typical fashion for parents of their generation, they managed to control most of their tears. But their good-bye hug was a little tighter and longer than any in my memory.

I remember feeling there was something good and very right about my spontaneous display of love toward my parents. Looking back, I think I grew up a little bit that day. As I backed the car out of the driveway and waved good-bye, I remember feeling happy that I had done what was right.

Another Story of Leaving Home

I feel fortunate that I grew up in a family full of love and support. As I grew into adulthood, it was natural for me to look for ways to return that love—to take responsibility to honor my parents for who they were and for what they had done for me. But I also recognize that many of you come from more unfortunate circumstances. Your relationship with your parents is much more difficult and complicated.

I once read another story of a child leaving home at age eighteen. It was just a bit different from mine.

After one of her messages, professional speaker Bobbie Gee was resting in a lounge, and a twenty-four-year-old woman with extremely short hair walked in. Bobbie complimented the woman on how her hair looked and was surprised at the reply: "Are you kidding?"

The woman proceeded to tell Bobbie that her hair was just growing back after being shaved for the removal of a brain tumor. She also was recovering from an extreme case of anorexia, which her doctors felt had helped cause the tumor.

And what circumstances led to the anorexia? "When I was eighteen years old, I came home from my high school graduation to find my bags packed and waiting on the front porch with a note from my dad that said I was now responsible for taking care of myself. It seems that all my dad lived for was getting us kids out of the home at eighteen."

Determined to somehow reach her unfeeling father, she managed to get arrested for shoplifting. That didn't work, so she stopped eating.

It wasn't until she lay in the hospital, near death from the anorexia, that her father finally came to see her. When he got up to leave, she began screaming, "You just can't say it, can you? I'm going to die and you still can't say it!"

"Say what?" he asked.

" 'I love you.' You never have, and I guess you never will."

These words finally shook the father. "My father returned to my hospital bed and began to cry like a baby when he realized that I had almost died and was willing to risk my life just to hear him tell me he loved me."

The woman's final comment was, "It's amazing the length some kids will go to try and get their parents to say, 'I love you.'"[1]

You Want Your Connection to Be Stronger

Many of us go our entire lives without fully understanding the connection we have with our parents. Whether you want to put your parents on a pedestal or leave them stranded on a deserted island, one thing is certain: Their words and actions have shaped you. They live in you. This is more than inheriting their mannerisms, their habits, or their values, and even more than DNA. You are connected to your parents at the deepest level of your soul.

Somewhere in your heart you wish you could reconnect.

Think of it this way: Some of you are proud to call your parents Mom and Dad, and you revel in that relationship. You want your connection to be stronger. Some of you don't know how to relate to them as you grow older. Sometimes you enjoy them, and sometimes they hurt and anger you. And the reason that pain is so acute is that you are connected to them. No matter what, you can't give up on the relationship; you, too, want that connection to be stronger.

And some of you feel nothing but pain when you think of your mother or father. You may have been abandoned. Perhaps you've been consistently mistreated or abused. Perhaps you have a parent who is evil and unrepentant. And yet for some mysterious reason, though you may never admit it to anyone, somewhere in your heart *you wish you could reconnect.*

That's the power of a parent.

Touching a Nerve

During my college years, my parents' humanity—and their mortality—became more and more real to me. I wrote some long letters to them expressing my thanks. I also used every opportunity when I was home to look Mom and Dad in the eyes and tell them I loved them.

During the early 1970s, I worked with teenagers in a ministry in Boulder, Colorado. One of my favorite messages to communicate to these teens was titled "How to Raise Your Parents." Actually, I camouflaged the real message behind the title. The real challenge was for these teenagers to obey God's fifth commandment, "Honor your father and your mother." As I spoke to those teenagers I realized that I was touching a raw nerve. Many had such difficult relationships with their parents that the command to honor them presented a challenge of immense proportions, a major step of faith.

As I have worked with youth and adults since then, I've realized that the church rarely talks about what it means to honor our parents. We'll talk about the need for children to obey their parents, but what does it mean for an adult child to honor them? The fifth commandment has become the forgotten commandment.

This is particularly puzzling because, for many of us, the relationship with a parent goes on for decades after we've left the nest. What does it look like to honor parents once you've become an independent adult?

During the 1980s, my interest in the forgotten commandment continued to grow. For several summers I taught a class about family to over five hundred students preparing for vocational ministry, and the lecture on honoring parents always brought the greatest response. I talked about honoring parents by thanking them, by forgiving them, by praising them, and by taking the initiative to build a relationship.

The responses were fascinating. After one lecture three young women came to me and described their dads, and each man sounded the same: successful in providing for material needs but aloof, detached, distant, and unexpressive. All three women had tears in their eyes as they expressed their desire to somehow build a loving relationship with their dads.

I counseled each woman to honor her father by taking the first step to change the relationship. "Don't expect your father to come to you, begging for your forgiveness," I said. "Instead, spend some time alone evaluating how you are responding to your father. Then, when appropriate, call your father; and if appropriate, confess to being ungrateful. Ask for forgiveness, and say, 'I love you.'"

Later I learned that, in each case, the father's heart melted. One woman told me, with tears streaming down her face, "For the first time in my life, my father and I communicated. In the past, my father gave me cars, jewelry, piano lessons, nice vacations, everything. I told him, 'I don't want all this stuff, I just want you. I love you and I want to know you.' He began to cry, and I began to cry. For the first time, he told me that he loved me.

"I don't think our relationship will ever be the same. I can't wait to go home."

"Something Is Happening Here"

Over the next few years, I continued to receive responses like that as I spoke to adult audiences on honoring their parents. I remember thinking, *God has something in this commandment we are missing today. He wants to do something profound in our relationship with our parents that I can't even begin to understand.*

Often when I've spoken on this subject I've shared a letter I received from a young woman, telling about the pain she had experienced in her family. Her letter vividly describes the payoff she received as she sought to honor her father:

> How thankful I am for the message you shared today. The truth of it rings loud and clear in my life.
>
> Growing up, my father physically abused me. Oh, he would beat me so bad that at times I didn't think I was going to live. At other times my mom would be in such fear for me that she would call the police.
>
> But perhaps even worse than the physical abuse was the

> mental abuse. Oh, how he hated me! He would cuss and scream at me every possible thing you could think of and a lot that you probably couldn't think of. I hated my father with a hate that few people probably ever realize exists.
>
> My freshman year in college I became a Christian. Over the next year and a half God took me from a tremendous hate of my father to a dislike to a like until I could say I loved my father.
>
> Then I began to find certain things out. My father was abused as a child. No one ever told me that before. His father kicked him out when he was seventeen.
>
> Does this excuse what happened to me as a child? No. Does it make it more understandable? Yes.
>
> My father still yells and cusses at me. But you know what? Not quite so loudly. I call him on special occasions. I share my life with him and ask his advice. His response? Not so good, but that's okay.
>
> The other day I heard he was bragging about me at work. There's hope. You know why there's hope? Because God loved us enough to send His Son to die on the cross for our sins, and because people like you care enough to share life-changing messages like you did today.

Most people would have counseled this young woman to turn her back on the father who physically abused her. "He's not deserving of your love," they'd say. And yet she chose to honor him anyway by expressing her love and giving him the hope of a relationship that he didn't deserve. When I hear stories like this, I realize that the commandment to honor our parents is far more important, and far more powerful, than most of us realize.

A Special Word to Children of Abusive Parents

As I dive into this topic of honoring parents, some of you will embrace the idea enthusiastically. Perhaps you have a good relationship with your parents. If so, you will probably enjoy applying some of the creative ideas you'll find in this book.

Some of you feel isolated from your parents or angry about how they've treated you. Perhaps you have trouble communicating with them, and you doubt whether it's even possible to establish a strong relationship. If you've been wounded deeply, the idea of honoring them seems impossible.

For some of you, reading this book will revive painful memories of a parent who abandoned you. Some of you suffered from physical, sexual, or emotional abuse. For you, the idea of honoring your parents is almost repugnant. You may feel intense anger just thinking about it. You may feel I don't understand your personal situation.

I have devoted one chapter, "When the Damage Goes Deep," specifically to people who have been abandoned or abused. In the meantime, let me gently encourage you to read through this book with an open heart. Ask God to show you how He would like you to respond to the fifth commandment.

I certainly have no desire to place on you a burden that you are unable to carry at this time. Perhaps it will be years before you can work through your pain. Perhaps you need time to work through serious issues from your family background with the help of counseling. But I have to believe that, tucked away in a quiet place in your soul, a part of you desperately desires a good relationship with your parents. If so, remember this: God is in the reconciliation business. It could be that taking steps to honor your parents will begin to pry open a rusty door in your relationship and let in a fresh wind of healing.

(2)

A PAINFUL LESSON

Appreciate your parents.
You never know what sacrifices
they went through for you.
—Anonymous

My personal odyssey with the concept of honoring our parents included one more discovery. It probably was the most significant of all . . . as well as the most painful.

When I spoke about honoring parents I would share practical ways to demonstrate that honor. The list included the usual: hugs, kisses, phone calls, texts, e-mails, cards, and handwritten letters. But I began to sense there had to be something more substantive than a phone call, more significant than a kiss or a hug, and more effective than a Mother's Day card. Even today, I can't fully explain it, but something started sprouting back in September of 1976, on the day my dad died.

Just a couple weeks earlier, Dad and Mom had visited us in Little Rock. Dad and I worked side by side, fixing up the house Barbara and I had recently purchased. We laughed as we went to the hardware store and asked for "quarter-inch putty," which we needed to fill in the space between the molding and ceiling. Neither of us was a handyman.

After they left to return home, I told Barbara it was one of the best times I'd ever had with Dad. Two weeks later my brother called. Dad had died of a massive heart attack.

He was gone. There were no warnings, no good-byes. As I stood by his casket a few days later, regret filled my soul. Why hadn't I expressed more of what I felt for him?

Did He Know How I Felt?

In the years that followed, I often reflected on Dad's funeral. Sixty-six years of his life, forty-four years of marriage, and forty-eight years of business were all summed up in a thirty-minute memorial. It was meaningful for our family, but it still bothered me; it seemed too brief a remembrance for all he meant to us.

Dad was a great man. Impeccable character. Quiet. Hard working. The most influential man in my life. It didn't seem right that a man's life could be summarized with such a superficial sketch.

I would not wait until Mom died to come to grips with her impact on my life.

I wondered, *Did he really know how I felt?* I had worked hard to express my love to him for several years, but words seemed so hollow. Had I really honored him as I should?

I pledged then that I would not wait until Mom died to come to grips with her impact on my life. I resolved to let her know about my feelings for her. A letter wouldn't do; it couldn't express my emotions adequately. What I had in mind had to be more personal. So I began working on a written tribute to her. I jotted down memories. Tears splattered on the legal pad as I recounted lessons she had taught me and fun times we had shared. It was an emotional catharsis.

Making It Special

Off and on for about a month I worked on her tribute. I crafted and honed every word, shaping each phrase with care and selecting memories that would honor her and bring a smile to her face.

When I finished it, I decided something was needed to set these words of honor apart from all the letters I had written in the past. With Barbara's help, I decided to have the tribute professionally laid out, printed, and framed. While personal, I also wanted it to look formal. I then shipped the finished product to Mom.

Here's what I wrote:

SHE'S MORE THAN SOMEBODY'S MOTHER

When she was thirty-five, she carried him in her womb. It wasn't easy being pregnant in 1948. There were no dishwashers or disposable diapers, and there were only crude washing machines. After nine long months, he was finally born. Breech. A difficult, dangerous birth. She still says, "He came out feet first, hit the floor running, and he's been running ever since." Affectionately she calls him "The Roadrunner."

A warm kitchen was her trademark—the most secure place in the home—a shelter in the storm. Her narrow but tidy kitchen always attracted a crowd. It was the place where food and friends were made! She was a good listener. She always seemed to have the time.

Certain smells used to drift out of that kitchen—the aroma of a juicy cheeseburger drew him like a magnet. There were green beans seasoned with hickory smoked bacon grease. Sugar cookies. Pecan pie. And the best of all, chocolate bonbons.

Oh, she wasn't perfect. Once when, as a mischievous three-year-old, he was banging pans together, she impatiently threw a pencil at him while she was on the phone. The pencil, much to her shock, narrowly missed his eye and left a sliver of lead in his cheek . . . it's still there. Another time she tied him to his bed because, when he was five years old, he tried to murder his teenage brother by throwing a gun at him. It narrowly missed his brother, but hit her prized antique vase instead.

She taught him forgiveness too. When he was a teenager she forgave him when he got angry and took a swing at her (and fortunately missed). The most profound thing she modeled was a love for God and people. Compassion was always her companion. She taught him about giving to others even when she didn't feel like it.

She also taught him about accountability, truthfulness, honesty, and transparency. She modeled a tough loyalty to his dad. He always knew divorce was never an option. And she took care of her own parents when old age took its toll. She also went to church . . . faithfully. In fact, she led this six-year-old boy to Jesus Christ in her Sunday evening Bible study class.

Even today, her age doesn't stop her from fishing in a cold rain, running off to get Chinese food, or "wolfing down" a cheeseburger and a dozen bonbons with her son.

She's truly a woman to be honored. She's more than somebody's mother . . . she's my mom.

Mom, I love you.

I knew she would like it, but I was unprepared for the depth of her appreciation. She hung it right above her table where she ate all her meals. There was only an old clock on another wall in that room, and that clock was no rival for my mom's tribute.

She shared it with family, the television repairman, the plumber, and countless others who passed through her kitchen. Later she told me, "On days when I'm down emotionally, I'll read that and think, *How can he write that about his mean, old mom?*" Seeing the tangible representation of my love on the wall above her breakfast table reminded her of the truth—what she did well as my mom.

My only regret is that I mailed it to her. Years later, Barbara personally read her tribute to her parents. Seeing that emotionally poignant moment with her parents unfold at Christmas was unforgettable. I wish I had driven home to Ozark with nothing else on my agenda other than to read my tribute to Mom—face-to-face, heart-to-heart, soul-to-soul—and to cry together with her.

Sharing the Idea with Others

The results of honoring Mom with a tribute were so encouraging that I began to challenge others to write tributes of their own. "Your parents need a tangible demonstration of your love *now.* Why wait until after they die to express how you feel?" I would ask.

Once again, I saw that something special happens when adults seek to connect with their parents by honoring them. People told me remarkable stories about the healing they had experienced in their relationships with parents. And in choosing to obey the forgotten commandment, many found that God was beginning a work of healing and growth in their own souls.

There is something great tucked away in this commandment.

My own personal pilgrimage, stretching back nearly six decades, tells me there is something great tucked away in this commandment. Perhaps your journey begins today.

For our next stop, let's see if we can begin to understand what God had in mind when He gave the command in the first place.

(3)

THE HEALING POWER OF HONOR: ONE MAN'S JOURNEY

You might say that Robert Lewis grew up in a twenty-first-century family . . . sixty years ago. He calls it the "modern family before it was modern."

In Ruston, Louisiana, in the 1950s, Robert's mom and dad got up each morning and headed off to work. Thomas Lewis sold insurance and Billie worked for a legal firm, where she became the personal assistant to the lieutenant governor and then to a state senator. While other children were cared for by full-time moms, Robert and his brothers spent a good part of their early years with live-in maids who cleaned the house, washed the clothes, and prepared the meals.

Robert's dad was never the type to show affection or approval. Robert never heard the words, "I love you" or "Great job!" Both parents were so busy that they didn't have much time for three small boys who needed daily encouragement and attention.

Still, Robert never thought his family was different—not until his dad started drinking heavily. By the time he turned ten, Robert knew something was terribly wrong in his home. His parents seemed to yell at each other all the time. As a teenager, he was frequently embarrassed in front of the friends he had brought home when finding his highly intoxicated dad stumbling through the house.

Christmas was often a disaster. His dad would usually drink himself through the holiday season. Although they weren't a religious family, Billie always wanted to gather the family for some religious observance, such as reading the nativity story from the Bible on Christmas Eve. But it never seemed to work out. Tensions would rise, the drinking would start, and then the screaming began. Three frightened and confused boys would sit watching as Christmas collapsed in chaos.

Robert does have some good memories. He recalls those infrequent fishing trips with his dad, when it was just father and son all day on a peaceful lake. His father could be such a delight when he was sober. And then there was that one autumn evening that, years later, remains a magical memory. The leaves were changing, the air was crisp, and both parents were in a good mood. Thomas was outside burning leaves while listening to a high school football game, and Billie was inside frying those oysters Robert loved.

There was just something so good about that moment. *This is how our family should be,* Robert thought. Yet, even then he knew it was just a moment in time.

Turning Point

Robert grew up with a lot of anger and resentment—which became an asset to him in fights and on the football field. He was mean.

"I saw in Jesus Christ someone I could entrust my life to, someone who would not leave or forsake me."

But he was also fortunate, because when he was fifteen one of his coaches took an interest in him. This coach stepped in and gave Robert much of the affirmation and encouragement he didn't get from his own father. He kept telling Robert, "You're a leader. You can do it. You can make decisions. You can be somebody special. I believe in you." Such encouragement worked wonders, and he excelled.

Robert received a football scholarship to the University of Arkansas. A neck injury prevented him from reaching his athletic potential, but something more significant happened during those college years when he became a follower of Christ. "I saw in Jesus Christ someone I could entrust my life to, someone who would not leave or forsake me. In Christ, I found stability and direction." After graduation, Robert attended Western Conservative Baptist Seminary in Portland, Oregon.

Like many children of alcoholics, Robert learned from an early age not to feel and not to think about the family's problems. He coped by burying his feelings and denying the reality of his family's dysfunction. But as he grew into adulthood and lived on his own, Robert started looking more realistically at his relationship with his parents. He began to realize just how much he had missed as a child. And he also realized he had to make a choice: He could blame his parents and seek revenge by criticizing them and isolating himself from them, or he could move toward forgiving them. In other words, he could play the role of victim, or he could take responsibility for the rest of his life.

Somehow, he began to look at his parents through a different lens. For years, he had focused on what they'd done wrong. Now that he was a husband and father himself, he saw how his own children didn't notice many of the good things he did for them. It dawned on him that he had forgotten many things his own parents had done right for him as well.

The Impossible Prayer

One night Robert was conducting a small-group Bible study in his home in Tucson, Arizona, where he was pastoring a church. To stimulate the discussion, Robert asked, "What is something that you would like to believe God for in prayer, but you just think is impossible?"

Each person answered the question, and when it was Robert's

turn he said, "I think it would probably be impossible for my dad to become a Christian." Thomas Lewis, then seventy years old, had lived his life without any interest in religion. Robert had explained the gospel to him twice, but each time Thomas refused to discuss it. "I'm not saying God couldn't do it," Robert told the group. "But it does feel hopeless. It seems almost impossible to pray for this." The evening concluded with prayer for all the "impossible" requests the group members had shared.

"I think it would probably be impossible for my dad to become a Christian."

Within twenty-four hours, Robert's world changed.

That very night, back in Louisiana, Robert's parents got into a terrible fight. Thomas was drunk and decided to leave the house. Billie, afraid to let Thomas drive, grabbed his shoulder. Thomas brushed her away, slammed the door behind him, and drove away in his car.

What Thomas didn't see was that when he brushed his wife's hand off his shoulder, she stumbled backward and fell against a marble coffee table. Her neck was fractured.

Billie lay on the floor, unable to move. Fortunately, a phone fell off the coffee table when she hit it, and an operator came on the line. Billie somehow forced out enough words to let the operator know she needed help.

Thomas stayed out all night and never even came home. Some friends found him at his office the next morning, and when they told him what had happened, he was so shocked he had a heart attack.

Robert didn't learn what had happened until the next morning, when a doctor called and said, "Your father has had a major heart attack. You need to come because he's probably not going to live long." Robert called a long-time friend to tell him he was coming home, and that was when he learned about his mother.

Reeling from those two blows, Robert boarded a plane in Tucson with a heavy heart. Would his dad live? Would his mom? And what was God doing here?

The Blessing

Robert arrived in Louisiana that night and drove immediately to the hospital. When he walked into his father's room, an amazing conversation began to unfold.

Thomas, groggy from medication, had a fuzzy look in his eyes. "How are you doing?" Robert asked. His dad replied, "Well, I'm not doing too good. I've done a horrible thing."

As Thomas began describing what he'd done, Robert realized his father was so medicated that he didn't recognize his own son. He thought he was talking to a doctor.

Then, as Robert listened, Thomas said, "Let me tell you about my three boys." He talked about where each of his sons lived and what they did, and then he got to Robert. "He talked about what a good son I was and that he was really proud of me . . . that I was pastor of this big church (he exaggerated) in Tucson."

For the first time in thirty years, Robert was hearing the words of praise and approval that a son needs to hear from his father.

As they kept talking, Thomas grew aware of who Robert was. "I've done a horrible thing," he cried. "I need to go to hell." Robert had never heard his father speak so directly about eternity, and without hesitating he replied, "Dad, that's where you're going to go if you don't come to the place of forgiveness in Christ."

"What do you mean?" Thomas asked. For the next hour Robert explained who Christ was, why He died on the cross, and how Thomas's sins could be forgiven. And that night, the impossible happened. Thomas ended years of independence and rebellion by praying with his son, confessing his sins and asking Christ to forgive him and come into his life as his Savior and Lord.

"I walked out, thinking, *This has got to be one of the greatest miracles I've ever witnessed, my dad coming to Jesus Christ and giving me the blessing on the same night.*" Robert recalls, "It was an incredible story. And, it all happened within twenty-four hours of a prayer that I thought God could never answer."

Reversing the Roles

As Robert's mother recovered in her hospital bed, she began to hear one regular chorus from her family and friends: Get a divorce. You've stayed with this man far longer than you should have. How could you possibly stay married to him after what he's done to you?

But Robert believed something good could come out of this tragedy. For the first time, his father had humbled himself and repented, and Robert knew this gave a glimmer of hope to the marriage. So he drew up a set of requirements for his dad:

- Never drink again.
- Seek professional counseling for your drinking.
- Live outside the home for an entire year to establish a track record of sobriety and recovery.

Robert took this list to his mother and asked, "If Dad can do all this, would you stay married and allow him back into your home after a year?" She didn't think it would happen, but she agreed to wait and see.

Then he approached his father and said, "Dad, you can either be responsible or you can be divorced. I can't stop the divorce, because Mom can choose that. She's got everybody on her side telling her to do that, but I will tell you that I got her to agree that if you will live responsibly, she will, in time, receive you back."

By standing up to his father and setting up conditions for the marriage continuing, Robert was, in a way, reversing the earlier roles of father and son. He was helping his dad take responsibility. And it worked—a year later his reborn father, clean and sober, moved back home.

"Some people would say that my parents had a miserable life," Robert says. "Well, they were inept in a lot of ways, and they certainly experienced a lot of pain. But when they finally had some help and some direction, they responded. It wasn't a perfect end, just a faithful one."

Writing a Tribute

A few years later Robert moved to Little Rock to be a pastor at my church. One Sunday morning Robert asked me to give the sermon, and I took the opportunity to speak about the forgotten commandment. I challenged the congregation to consider honoring their parents with a written tribute—a document thanking and honoring them for what they did right as parents.

Even though Robert and I had developed a good friendship, I had no idea of the drama that surrounded his family and how he would apply this message to his parents. But the idea of honoring his parents germinated in his mind for a couple years until he found himself with a free afternoon during a retreat in Colorado.

He had confronted his feelings of bitterness and had forgiven his parents years before.

He had confronted his feelings of bitterness and had forgiven his parents years before, but now his parents were getting on in age. Robert sensed he ought to put together something special for them.

He took a pen and some paper, sat in the ski lodge in front of a fire, and began to write down some recollections from his childhood. To his surprise, a flood of memories started coursing through his mind—the terrible moments of his childhood as well as the happy ones, all the anger and joy and sadness and longing. The explosion of emotion overwhelmed him; he thought he was just going to sit down and write an easy letter, but here he was weeping as he never had before. People were staring at him, and soon he had to return to his room.

For the next four hours, Robert released much of the pain he had built up through the years. "It's hard to describe," Robert says, "because I've always been more of a cerebral type. To have this flood of emotion was getting in touch with a part of myself that I didn't even know was there. The closet door came open and all this stuff flooded out. It was powerful and potent. And bittersweet. But it was also thrilling, because I felt the healing winds of freedom within me."

When he was finished, he had written a document he titled "Here's to My Imperfect Family." It's a startling title, but he felt he couldn't paint a rosy picture of the past; his family was too honest for that. They knew the trials they had gone through, but at the same time, Robert wanted to remind them of the good things he had discovered in a fresh way.

A Christmas Ceremony

Robert had the document typeset and framed, and on Christmas Day he and his family drove down to Ruston. After all the other gifts were opened, he stood up and said, "There are a lot of things I've always wanted to say to you that I've not known how to say. So I've tried my best to put it into writing and I'd like to read it to you." With his wife and four children standing by his side, he read the following tribute:

HERE'S TO MY IMPERFECT FAMILY

When I think of family, I think first of you, Mama, and you, Daddy. I will never understand the forces that drew or held you two together all these years. Clearly it has not been easy. But then again, I have now learned that few marriages are. Each carries its own crucible. Reflecting back as one of your three sons, it's not hard to say that our family was less than perfect. The "imperfect family" would be a much more descriptive term for our home. To be sure, we never had enough or did enough together. We fell short of many ideals. . . .

Those things have little, if any, hold on me now. Instead, I frequently recall "particular" things that are now forever imbedded within me . . . things that need to be stated in writing, for they are the secret successes of my imperfect family.

I am glad you never divorced. Today I do not think of a way out because you never got out. My children know about divorce from their friends but not from their family. They will grow up carrying permanency in marriage in their heritage; and though that in itself will not ensure success for them . . . it will help as it helped me.

I am more appreciative than ever for your sacrificial involvement and investment in me. I will never know them all, as my children will never know all of mine. But I do know some.

Your presence at my school programs and Little League games is one. Responding to late night fever and upset stomachs and crises like the "chicken bone affair" . . . caught in the throat of a frightened third grader. I needed you, Mom, and you were there. I also remember the genuine compassion I received after being heartbroken that I stood and watched rather than starred in my first organized football game. And the hours you expended talking with me . . . exploring and surfacing my thoughts, feelings, and ambitions. How that helped!

I think of fishing at Kepler's Lake with Daddy. Boy, was that fun! I still enjoy it every time I relive it. And through your help for a young black man named James, I have a deeper social consciousness toward those "not like me." And thanks, Daddy, for saying "I'm sorry" when you wrongfully hit me in anger one day. You don't remember the incident, I know, but I do. It's deep inside me now . . . and it comes back to me every time I need to say those words to my children and my wife. Seeing that day in my mind makes that humbling process easier.

I owe both of you a thousand "thank-yous" . . . for Florida vacations at the Driftwood Lodge . . . for all the oysters I could eat on my birthday . . . for the constant encouragement during teenage years . . . for teaching me about inner toughness. I can still hear it. "If you can't take it, you can always quit" . . . for struggling in December to give Christmas its real meaning. Mom, I get the picture now . . . for teaching Sunday school at Trinity . . . for traveling to all those ball games . . . for standing behind me when I turned LSU down . . . for saying I love you because I needed to hear it . . . for the new car in college (I know some of how that must have hurt now) . . . for not panicking when it seemed your son had become a religious fanatic . . . for letting me know the financial "ride" was over after college and I was on my own . . . for not getting too involved in shaping my direction . . .

There is much more, of course. Much more. I guess if I were offered one wish, it would be for one day of childhood in time past . . . when I could again be your little boy. It would be a crisp fall evening with the smell of burning leaves and a Bearcat game in the air. I would be outside enjoying the bliss of youthful innocence. Mom, you would be frying those oysters, and, Daddy, you would be crooning out the words, "My goodness, gracious Toddy!"

So here's to my imperfect family. One that fell short in many respects, but one whose love makes the shortcomings easy to forget. Here's to the family that never had it all together but one just perfect enough . . . for me!

I love you,
Robert

Robert had to stop several times because of the flood of tears. He remembers seeing his dad sitting there with his eyes welling up, too. He couldn't bring himself to cry, but it was obviously touching him deeply. His mom was stunned. She sat there, silently weeping tears of happiness.

When it was over, they all sat there for a moment in sweet silence. They weren't used to hearing such transparent words in the Lewis family. And now nobody knew what to say.

However, when Robert walked into his parents' home the next day, the first thing he saw was the framed tribute, hung in the most prominent spot in the house. "We all knew the imperfections and warts," Robert says, "but, here in this tribute, my mother and dad had finally been honored for what they did right. And it was wonderful."

That was December of 1985. Just nine months later, Thomas died of a heart attack. Yet for Robert, the pain of that moment was eclipsed by a deeper chorus of positive feelings.

Standing before his father's open casket, Robert remembers thinking, *There is nothing I wish I would have said to you, Dad, because I said it. "I have no regrets. I am healed, and, now, so are you.*

"We can both rest in peace."

(4)

WHAT IS HONOR?

What is honored in a land will be cultivated there.

—Plato

Who receives honor in our culture today?

Sports heroes receive honor. If you can dunk a basketball, knock the breath out of a running back, or throw a baseball ninety-five miles per hour, you can make millions of dollars in contracts and endorsements.

Entertainers receive honor. Hardly a week goes by without some television show presenting some type of award to music, television, and movie performers.

Soldiers, firefighters, and police officers earn acclaim and medals for acts of courage and heroism. Employees often are honored for top performances or for years of service to a company.

And what usually accompanies the honor? Pomp and pageantry. Applause. Photographs. A handshake. Hugs. Public recognition and words of appreciation.

Ever watch someone receive an honor who was not expecting it?

You see shock, gratitude, and appreciation streak across his face. And chances are he'll never forget the moment.

I'll tell you who does not receive much honor in our culture: those in authority. Our culture has declared open season on authority figures. Our leaders have become easy prey for the daily techno-feast of the vultures on the web and on the television news. One wonders if Washington or Lincoln could have escaped the carnage today's media creates.

Fewer people are willing to take on the job of parenting when it has so little honor attached to it.

In addition, leaders of businesses, churches, and organizations face a steady barrage of dishonor from the crushing demands and expectations of those he or she directs. I suspect the crisis we are experiencing with a shortage of competent leadership could be traced to the fact that thinking men and women are simply unwilling to risk the likelihood of public dishonor that comes from stepping to the front of the pack.

I'm most disturbed, though, by the general lack of honor given to perhaps the most important segment of our society: parents. One wonders if the decline in the birth rate over the last few decades reflects this problem; fewer people are willing to take on the job of parenting when it has so little honor attached to it.

Now, it's true that each year on Mother's Day and Father's Day, you'll find a temporary burst of stories in the media on parenthood. A national magazine asks celebrities, "What lessons did you learn from your father?" A television reporter features his mother and tells his audience about her love and sacrifice.

And then, during the rest of the year, we see the other side. We read of celebrities revealing how their parents abused them as kids, of adults blaming their parents for their problems—from alcoholism to repressed sexuality to overeating. We see television sitcoms where parents are portrayed as incompetent buffoons.

We have become a nation of dishonor. And no nation, no person, ever moves forward in a milieu of dishonor.

Honor: A Weighty Matter

Honor, according to Webster's Dictionary, is "a good name or public esteem. A showing of unusual merited respect." When God commands us to "honor your father and your mother," however, He provides some additional meaning. In the original Hebrew language, the word for *honor* meant "heavy" or "weighty." Its literal meaning was "to lay it on them." When we use that phrase—lay it on them—we typically mean flattery. Not so here. To honor someone meant "I weigh you down with respect and prestige. I place upon you great worth and value."

Think of the setting when God gave Israel the Ten Commandments. God had brought this nation of people, held captive for so long in Egypt, into the wilderness of Sinai. He had promised them the land of Israel, but up to this point He had never given them any written directions. They needed a constitution that would teach them how to relate to God and how to live with one another. They needed instructions to govern their behavior and preserve their identity as a nation.

So it's critical to understand the significance of the command to honor parents. Note where it falls in the list of Ten Commandments (based on Exodus 20:3–17):

1. You shall have no other gods before me.
2. You shall not make for yourself a carved image, or any likeness of anything that is in the heaven above, or that is in the earth beneath . . . You shall not bow down to them or serve them, for I the LORD your God am a jealous God.
3. You shall not take the name of the LORD your God in vain.
4. Remember the Sabbath day, to keep it holy.

5. Honor your father and your mother, that your days may be long in the land that the LORD your God is giving you.
6. You shall not murder.
7. You shall not commit adultery.
8. You shall not steal.
9. You shall not bear false witness against your neighbor.
10. You shall not covet your neighbor's house; you shall not covet your neighbor's wife, or . . . anything that is your neighbor's.

I believe God had a purpose for placing the fifth commandment where He did. By doing so, He highlighted two important truths about honoring parents.

1. Honoring your parents should grow out of a strong relationship with God.

Note that the first four commandments deal with how humans relate to God. With these mandates, God established that He is the One who should be exalted above anyone or anything else. Then comes the fifth commandment. This tells me that honoring parents should be a direct result of our faith in Him.

Look carefully at the commandment again. Whom did God command us to honor? Only perfect parents? Only Christian parents? Parents who are spiritually mature and insightful? Only parents who never made major mistakes in rearing us? No, God commands us to honor our parents regardless of their performance, behavior, and dysfunction. Why? Because honoring parents demands that we live by faith.

For some of you, honoring your parents may be a "spiritual barometer" of your relationship with God. Do you want to walk in His ways and experience His love and power? Then you need to obey His commands. In John 15:10 Jesus said, "If you keep my commandments, you will abide in my love, just as I have kept my Father's commandments, and abide in his love."

God knew we needed to live by faith, to be obedient to Him without always understanding the reason for everything we do. For some, honoring your parents will stretch your faith. You will do it only because God commanded it, not because you feel your parents deserve it. But you will grow spiritually in the process because you have exercised faith.

One other important truth to remember is that God did not leave us powerless to obey this commandment. Deuteronomy 30:11 states, "For this commandment that I command you today is not too hard for you, neither is it far off."

This may seem preposterous, because no human being in history, except for Christ, has ever been able to obey the Ten Commandments perfectly. But that is why God gave us the Holy Spirit—to give us the power to obey Him. Look at these encouraging words from John 14:15–17.

> If you love me, you will keep my commandments. And I will ask the Father, and he will give you another Helper, to be with you forever, even the Spirit of truth, whom the world cannot receive, because it neither sees him nor knows him. You know him, for he dwells with you and will be in you.

If you have received Christ as your Lord and Savior, God has given you His Helper, who can empower you to fulfill God's commandments.

2. *Honoring your parents should be a key cornerstone of a nation.*

By divine decree, the fifth commandment to honor your parents was listed before the remaining directives about murder, adultery, stealing, lying, and coveting. In establishing this new nation, God assigned priority status to the institution of the family and its relationships. He makes a clear statement: Do you want your nation to thrive for a long

- Acknowledging the sacrifices they have made for you
- Praising them for the legacy they are passing on to you
- Seeing them through the eyes of Christ, with understanding and compassion
- Forgiving them as Christ has forgiven you

Honor is an attitude accompanied by actions that say to your parents, "You are worthy. You have value. You are the person God sovereignly placed in my life. You may have failed me, hurt me, and disappointed me, but I am taking off my judicial robe and releasing you from the courtroom of my mind. I choose to look at you with compassion; as a person with needs, concerns, and scars of your own."

Honoring Parents Brings Rewards

Renowned soprano Marian Anderson was asked by a reporter to name the greatest moment in her life. She could have chosen from a long list of significant accomplishments. There was the night the famous conductor Toscanini told her that hers was the finest voice of the century. There was the private concert she gave at the White House for the Roosevelts and the king and queen of England. She had received the Bok Award as the person who had done the most for her hometown of Philadelphia. And to top it all, there was that Easter Sunday in Washington when she stood beneath the Lincoln Memorial and sang for a crowd of 75,000, including cabinet members, Supreme Court justices, and members of Congress.

Which of those big moments did she choose?

None.

She said the greatest moment in her life was the day she went home and honored her mother by telling her that she wouldn't have to take in washing anymore to pay the bills.[2]

As Marian Anderson learned, honoring your parents may be one of the most rewarding and memorable deeds of your life.

5 WAYS TO HONOR YOUR PARENTS BY BUILDING YOUR RELATIONSHIP

1. **Become a student of your parents.** Learn what communicates value, respect, and esteem to them. Do they value phone calls, letters, or visits on family holidays? Then make those a priority.

If their birthdays are important to them, make sure you send cards and gifts on time. If you have hurt them by not attending a key family gathering, make a special effort to be there next time.

If they have special skills, you can honor them by asking for their assistance and advice. If your father is good at carpentry, for example, ask him to help you build those new bookshelves you have been wanting for your den.

2. **Give them your time.** My guess is that your parents value your time more than anything else.

Through our own sets of mistakes, Barbara and I have found that if we want to honor our parents as a way of life, we've had to lose a bit of our independence. It's not always convenient to spend time with your parents.

Look for some common interests you can develop. Your father may enjoy fishing, golfing, or watching professional baseball games. Arrange for a weekend fishing trip or take him to a local golf course and pay for the green fees yourself. Or drive over one night to watch the World Series with him.

Your mother would likely appreciate help around her home—like spending a weekend painting a room or two, or working in the yard to help with upkeep. Whether it's going out to lunch, going shopping, or going on a weekend road trip together, the point is to invest some of your time back in her direction.

3. **Take vacations with them.** In 1990, my family spent a long vacation on a lake in northern Minnesota. Barbara's parents joined us for a few days, and there's no question that those days did a lot to cement the relationship. One day we ended up with a van full of memories as all ten of us spent over twelve hours together. We toured the port at Duluth, a huge iron ore mine, and a beautiful high school in Hibbing. We reminisced as Barbara's dad showed us where he vacationed as a boy with his family. It really turned out to be a great day, filled with memories.

4. **Seek their advice.** If you are about to purchase a home for the first time, for example, let them help you by giving you advice. Not only will you show respect, but you also might avoid some costly mistakes.

If you feel your parents are too critical of your choices, you will need to be cautious here. I would let them know you are not putting yourself back under their authority, but taking advantage of their experience and their wisdom on major issues.

Sometimes it's risky to seek your parents' counsel because you may decide to go a totally different direction. These risks are real and disagreement can occur. If this happens, aggressively seek to honor them and explain that you really appreciated their advice, but that in the end, you really needed to do something totally different.

5. **Write letters.** I don't want to minimize the importance of regular phone calls, video calls, e-mails, or text messages. But

one of the best things you can do is to resurrect the art of letter writing. There is something special about sitting down and writing a letter that communicates in a way that a phone call never can. Snoopy, the character in the comic strip *Peanuts* by Charles Schulz, reminds us, "Nothing echoes like an empty mailbox." Handwritten letters are increasingly a statement of true love, appreciation, and honor.

(5)

THE PROMISE

When I was a boy of fourteen, my father was so ignorant I could hardly stand to have the old man around. But when I got to be twenty-one, I was astonished at how much the old man had learned.

—Mark Twain

Lien Mersha was only five when her parents were killed in an automobile accident. When she lost her family, something inside her died as well.

"I started stuttering, didn't talk until spoken to, never talked to kids, never played outside," Lien says. "I'd come home after school and go to my room."

Labeled a problem child, Lien lived in fourteen different foster homes during the next six years. She shoplifted, broke windows, pulled pranks on neighbors, and began taking drugs. "I was always in trouble. They told me I was going to end up in jail. I believed it for a long time."

And then she met Nhon and My Le.

In April of 1975, Nhon was a pilot in the South Vietnamese Air Force. On one of the last, hectic days before Communist North Vietnam took control of the country, Nhon and My fled the country with their two young children, Dat and Tuyen. After a few months in a refugee camp, the family was allowed to emigrate to the United States.

"I started crying and saying, 'I didn't know you loved me.'"

Nhon and My were both committed Christians, and they wanted to give something back to the country that had given them a new life. They wanted to do something that would make a statement of appreciation to their new homeland. So they approached the state social services agency and asked for the worst case they had.

The social worker came up with several possible children, but in each case Nhon and My shook their heads and told the astounded social worker the child was not bad enough! They really wanted a needy, problem child.

They ended up with Lien.

When Lien learned that her new foster family was Vietnamese, she thought it was a joke. But something was different this time. No matter what she did, Nhon and My stuck with her. "They went through hell and back with me," Lien says. "Dad said it was almost like getting shot at by the enemy. They took shot after shot after shot. I would keep shooting bullets at him that never really harmed him because he knew, in the end, there would be so much good that would come out in me."

The turning point came one evening during a conflict. Nhon said, "Lien, why do you take the love I have for you away?"

For the first time, Lien realized someone actually loved her. "I started crying and saying, 'I didn't know you loved me.' I began to realize that the Les were important to me and that if I continued doing drugs, I would lose them. I realized I had something special here and I needed to make it work."

After that, Lien began to change. She decided she would honor her parents by obeying them and trying to please them. She agreed to go through treatment for her drug problem. They told her about their faith in Christ, and at age seventeen she received Him into her life at a church retreat.

A couple of years later, a newspaper reporter sat down to a meal at a Vietnamese restaurant and was surprised to see that her waitress was a blonde-haired, blue-eyed teenager, Lien. She was even further intrigued when she learned that Lien's parents were the Vietnamese owners of the restaurant. She arranged for an interview, and that gave Lien the opportunity to write a tribute for her parents.

The newspaper printed the entire tribute verbatim. Here are some excerpts.

> When my father came here five years ago, he started as a kitchen cleaner, a housekeeper, a butcher. He worked for $2.05 an hour. He worked as a keypunch operator, then advanced to a programmer. Now he's a system programmer, owns his own restaurant, and is the owner of a five-bedroom colonial home in Southeast Minneapolis. Last year they both became American citizens. They have helped 11 people come over here from Vietnam.
>
> I treasure them so. They can never do any wrong in my eyes.
>
> My mom worked for Control Data before they started the restaurant. I can talk to her about anything. I admire the way she always stands behind my father in his decisions and supports him. They knew I was on drugs, but they wanted to help me. They took a chance that nobody else would. They saw that I wanted to be good—that in order for me to be good, I had to be around good surroundings.
>
> I don't mind authority now. I think it's everything in the way they show me they care. If I have a problem, it's theirs. No

> matter what time of the day, I can go to them and say if I've a problem and they take time for me. It doesn't matter what they're doing. They always stop and talk to me.
>
> Nobody has ever taken the risks that my parents have with me. They trust me to run the restaurant. They trust me with their cars. They trust me with their children Dat and Tuyen.
>
> The kids are very precious to me. I have so much insight now for when I raise my own family . . . things I'd do differently. I'd want them to know that when they're in trouble with me, I don't hate them and don't like disciplining them. I'm doing it because they made a decision and even though it isn't right, they're responsible for the outcome.
>
> The main thing is that [they] have shown me that there is a chance. I've seen a life now that I want—that I didn't want before. I've learned the past will never leave you, but you don't have to worry about it because it's gone. It's the present and the future that you have to look forward to.

Today Lien is married and is even raising adopted children of her own. "We hope one of our children will adopt when they're older and carry on their grandparents' legacy," she says.

Lien Mersha is a walking miracle. But her remarkable story demonstrates more than the power of loving and committed parents. It also illustrates a remarkable truth of Scripture: When you honor your parents, God gives you a tremendous blessing. Her life began to change when she finally began to honor the parents who demonstrated so much love to her.

The First Command with a Promise

If honoring your parents is the forgotten commandment, then the second half of the fifth commandment must be the forgotten blessing. In the last chapter I addressed the first half of Exodus 20:12, and now I'd like to discuss the second: "Honor your father and your mother, *that your days may be long in the land that the LORD your God is giving you*" (emphasis added). Deuteronomy 5, another list of the Ten Commandments, adds the phrase, "that it may go well with you in the land that the LORD your God is giving you." None of the other Ten Commandments has a promise attached to it. Paul even mentioned in Ephesians 6:2 that this is "the first commandment with a promise."

But what does it mean? How can your days be prolonged by honoring parents? In what ways will it "go well with you"?

Deuteronomy 30 contains some pretty specific promises, and they boil down to this: If you obey God's commandments, He will bless you. If you disobey Him, He will withdraw those benefits:

> See, I have set before you today life and good, death and evil. If you obey the commandments of the LORD your God that I command you today, by loving the LORD your God, by walking in his ways, and by keeping his commandments and his statutes and his rules, then you shall live and multiply . . . But if your heart turns away . . . I declare to you today, that you shall surely perish. . . . Therefore choose life, that you and your offspring may live, loving the LORD your God, obeying his voice and holding fast to him, for he is your life and length of days. (vv. 15–20)

Do you want to live your life with the favor of God upon you? Would you like to feel the blessing and the good hand of God upon your life? Then obey His commands.

I've heard enough stories to convince me that the commandment to honor parents can transform your life. Obviously, if we honor our parents, there are the benefits of better communication, the possibility of peace with them, and greater freedom in our relationship with them. But I believe there are some hidden benefits as well. This promise is one of the most mysterious and powerful in all of Scripture.

The next chapter will focus on how you and your legacy will benefit from being connected by honor to your parents, and chapter 7 will explain how your parents will profit with a better relationship from your act of honoring them. But let's first consider another profound way that "it will go well with you." Honoring your parents will help you finish the process of growing up into adulthood.

Putting Away Childishness

In 1 Corinthians 13:11, Paul wrote of our need to grow up: "When I was a child, I spoke like a child, I thought like a child, I reasoned like a child. When I became a man, I gave up childish ways." Paul knew that kids will be kids; they will behave childishly. But he also implied that, as we grow up, we must set aside childish behavior and become mature.

Children, in relationships, are by nature petty, hurtful, and fault finding. They speak rashly, rudely, and selfishly, with little thought of how their words will affect their parents. They think they are always right and others are wrong, even when the evidence has declared them guilty.

Paul's challenge is to lay aside our childishness and finish the process of becoming an adult. A part of maturing as an adult is the growing realization and conviction that you are just as responsible for the relationship as your parents are. If your parents are elderly or are in poor health, you may be even more responsible than they are for the relationship.

For most of your first eighteen to twenty years of life, your relationship with your parents could be compared to a one-way street. She nursed you and changed your diapers; he walked the floor with you at 2:00 a.m. She taught you how to walk; he taught you how to drive.

The traffic of love generally flowed in one direction. And it probably remained that way through high school and college. The problem with some parent-child relationships, however, is they continue moving only one way even when the child is in his thirties and forties. The adult child fails to assume his responsibility of making the relationship a two-way street. He remains passive, letting his parents take the initiative and setting the rules for the relationship.

A Rite of Passage

"I never felt my mother treated me like an adult."

Sound familiar? How often have you felt the same way about your parents? How often have your friends echoed those words?

That statement came from Elizabeth, who otherwise seemed happy with her life. She lived in the same town as her mother, but it all seemed so strained and shallow. "She and I had a fairly cold, awkward relationship. We would very rarely laugh together. I would have a hard time letting my guard down with her, and she would have a hard time letting her guard down with me."

"Honoring her was a concrete way of forgiving her."

When they talked, the conversation always centered on superficial things, like how work was going or what the kids were doing. "We wouldn't talk about feelings at all. She still treated me and my other siblings a lot like kids. I felt a lack of respect," Elizabeth explained.

To Elizabeth's mother, there was one way to do things, her way. "There was no respect for our ideas, even on things like what we ate for dinner or what clothes we picked out."

Over the years, Elizabeth began to withdraw from her mother. She saw her every couple of weeks, but she removed herself emotionally. For a while she didn't feel as if she was missing anything. But her feelings began to change shortly after she heard the idea of honoring her parents and writing a tribute for them. She wrestled with the idea for two years.

Finally she realized she needed to take action. "I had dwelt on the negative for so long. There was a wall between us. It was just one of those things I knew I needed to do."

As she worked on the tribute and remembered good things her mom had done for her, she felt God slowly give her a different perspective on her mom. "I think as I was going through it I learned to appreciate her more than I had. I always wondered what it meant to honor her in the midst of all these negative things that had happened. Even though she did things wrong, I felt I needed to forgive my mom. Honoring her was a concrete way of forgiving her."

While Elizabeth was working on her tribute, she and her mother had a big argument. "I was very, very angry with her. It was a really big decision to still do the tribute, even in the middle of this argument. With my husband's encouragement and God giving me the courage, I went ahead and finished it and gave it to Mom on Christmas."

As her mother read the tribute, to Elizabeth's surprise, she immediately broke down in tears. "I think part of the problem was that all those years, while I was feeling she didn't respect me, she didn't feel any respect and appreciation from her kids."

The tribute allowed Elizabeth and her mother to set aside their argument and begin building their relationship. "I feel like she's more relaxed with me. I feel like there have been some walls broken down. The other day she called and we were laughing about something on the phone. My husband heard us and said, 'I just can't believe how much your relationship with your mom has changed.' "

I really saw how fruitful obedience to God and His commands can be.

Even though her mother appreciated the tribute, it may have meant more to Elizabeth. "In a way, it was for me as much as anything else. I knew it was something that God wanted me to do, but I really didn't know all the positive benefits that were going to come out of it. I really saw how fruitful obedience to God and His commands can be.

"It's been hard for my siblings to deal with how I handled this. They are not Christians, and they have absolutely no understanding of why I would ever look at these good things that my parents did.

"I'm not sure how to deal with that. I do know that I felt like the kid all the time, but after I did that tribute, I felt like I was more on Mom's level. I was able to relate to her more. It was sort of a rite of passage."

Ending the Standoff

You may find yourself facing problems very similar to Elizabeth's. You are waiting for your parents to respect you, recognize you as an adult, and let you go. And your parents are waiting for you to honor them.

It's a standoff.

And only when you choose to take responsibility for your part of the relationship will you begin to establish yourself as a mature adult, both in your parents' eyes and in your own.

I can see at least three reasons why this maturing process begins to occur.

First, honoring your parents requires you to take initiative in the relationship. I will not pretend that the process of honoring parents is the total answer to a lack of self-confidence or identity crisis in a man or a woman. Nor can I guarantee it will mark the decisive turning point in a relationship with parents. But I have heard and read enough stories to recognize something mysterious happens in men and women who reach out to honor their parents. Perhaps it's because the act of honoring demands that we initiate and give. Regardless, it's significant when a forty-five-year-old business executive reveals that honoring his parents helped him become identified as a man and feel like an adult for the first time in his life. It changed the dynamics of his relationship with them.

Second, honoring your parents helps you set aside the victim mentality. It's an old idea, but it seems to be in vogue these days: "It's not my fault!" The idea is that your problems and flaws result from your environment rather than from personal choices. Pop psychology de-emphasizes the concept of personal responsibility; after all, we don't want to feel guilty for the wrong choices we make, do we? Instead we are encouraged to blame others—often our parents—for our difficulties.

I'm reminded of the story of a little boy who came home from school with another bad report card. When he handed the report to his dad, the boy looked him in the eye and asked, "What do you think it is this time—heredity or environment?"

I need to state clearly that many people are indeed victims. I cannot deny that many emotional or relational difficulties adults face can be traced to parents who either abandoned their children or who abused and damaged them emotionally.

Honoring your parents helps you mature by taking a hard, honest look at them.

What is happening in our culture, however, is that too many people are blaming and bashing parents while using their victim status to avoid a prickly question: When am I going to be responsible for my own life? Maturity and adulthood begin to occur because honoring your parents moves you away from being the victim toward a new perspective, taking responsibility for your life and for your relationship with your parents.

Third, honoring your parents helps you mature by taking a hard, honest look at them. Many adult children have spent their lifetime denying the truth about their parents. All these negative emotions have been conveniently captured and buried where we don't have to face the reality, thinking they will not bother us. But when memories and emotions are buried, we are unable to deal honestly with them. And maturity demands us to confront our past, our circumstances, and our emotions. An individual will never experience the benefits of growing up if he or she is denying and refusing to face the reality of having been raised by fallen human beings.

When I encourage adults to go through the process of honoring their parents by writing a tribute, I suggest they sit down over a period of days to collect memories—both the good and the bad. This surfaces a lot of emotions, including appreciation, joy, love, anger, bitterness, and disappointment. Often the negative emotions hold the positive memories captive. But if they get honest with themselves, many people will end up with a more complete view of their parents. It helps them grieve over the mistakes and pain while also acknowledging what their parents did right. And that can lead to healing.

Leave the Results to God

God is challenging us to grow up by honoring our parents. He is calling us to responsible, thoughtful acts of love toward those He says we must honor.

Remember, you are not accountable for your parents' response. Your parents may refuse your love and honor. They may not forgive you for your mistakes. They may never ask you to forgive them for how they have hurt you. Your responsibility is to obey God, and let Him work in their hearts.

One woman wrote me:

> Please tell people that not everyone will have a happy miracle to tell after calling their mother or father (or both) and asking forgiveness. Two months ago I decided that was the step I needed to take with my father, so I called him and very humbly apologized and asked him to forgive me. He would not. I was attacked verbally and made to feel very guilty. The conversation ended in tears. My comfort is not in a happy ending—yet—but in knowing that I have obeyed my God.

But her story didn't end there. Before she sent me the letter she happened to talk with her father again. She added this postscript:

> I just got off the phone with my father—I didn't think my happy ending would come so soon. My father's world is crashing in around him—he declared bankruptcy yesterday.
>
> As a result I lost my place to live at school next year and I will have to postpone my senior year so I can work full time. A number of other comforts have also been denied.
>
> But as I talked to my father I found that I had no bitter feelings, no hatred, and no anger. Instead I heard myself asking him if there was anything I could do for him—I felt compassion and concern. And when I started to say goodbye, I heard myself tell my father, "I love you."

Our Lord's words in James 4:6 are true: "God opposes the proud, but gives grace to the humble." This woman realized that in order to honor her father and create a two-way street, she needed to humble herself and ask for forgiveness. Even though she didn't receive the forgiveness she desired, I believe that step of faith may have changed their relationship. She became a giver instead of a taker. She put away childish things and began relating to her father as an adult.

(6)

A LIFELINE TO YOUR LEGACY

What a father says to his children
is not heard by the world,
but it will be heard by posterity.
—Jean Paul Richter

I am part of the Baby Boom generation, and I grew up in an era when authority was challenged. We invented the term "generation gap," warning ourselves never to trust anyone over thirty. We believed old values and old morals were outdated. Now we are the older generation and our own children and grandchildren are calling *us* outdated!

I heard a story about a teenage grandson who, along with his parents, was visiting his grandmother. The teenager began discussing male/female roles with his grandmother and argued that her ideas were old-fashioned. What really hurt the grandmother, though, was watching her own daughter and son-in-law encouraging their son. "It felt to me like they were cheering him on," she said. Her concluding comment illustrates what happens when we fail to honor parents: "I feel no link to him."

The Wisdom of the Past

The link between generations is a precious thing. It's clear in Scripture that God's most important structure for passing along timeless spiritual truths is the family—parents teaching their children, grandparents teaching their grandchildren, and so on. Read these words from Psalm 78:5–7.

> He established a testimony in Jacob and appointed a law in Israel, which he commanded our fathers to teach to their children, that the generation might know them, the children yet unborn, and arise and tell them to their children, so that they should set their hope in God and not forget the works of God, but keep his commandments.

God calls each generation to pass spiritual truth on to the next. For the family to carry on this type of spiritual relay, they must maintain a multigenerational connection. This is the second way that life "will go well with you" (Deuteronomy 5:30); by honoring your parents you enable the legacy of one generation to continue unbroken to the next.

If you read through Proverbs, you'll recognize the priority God places on the connection of children to their parents. Through this connection children learn the discipline and wisdom needed for life. Proverbs 3:1–2, for example, says, "My son, do not forget my teaching, but let your heart keep my commandments, for length of days and years of life and peace they will add to you."

When the elderly are ignored rather than honored, when we start believing there is nothing children can learn from parents or grandparents, we cut ourselves off from the wisdom of the past.

The Power of Legacy

Here's something to ponder: If you died right now, how would your children, friends, and family describe the legacy of your life? What would they say about you?

Now, stop and consider your parents. What positive statements could be said of their lives? What kind of legacy have they left you? What is worth passing on to the next generation?

By honoring your parents for their positive contributions in your life, you highlight the legacy of their lives. You bring value and dignity to human beings who may have never been successful by the world's standards. You pass on to succeeding generations stories of lessons learned and wisdom gathered.

Honoring parents keeps a legacy alive in three ways.

First, it allows you to learn from your parents. If you have godly parents, this is not difficult for you to understand. But if your parents are not believers, or if they have failed in their roles as parents in the past, you may have a hard time believing your parents have something to offer you.

It could be, in many areas, you have gained greater wisdom than your parents. But how many of you can really say that there is *absolutely nothing* you can learn from them? I have yet to meet a person who can honestly say he knows everything he needs about how to live. It could be you need to look for ways to draw upon your parents' advice.

Perhaps there isn't any spiritual legacy in your family, but is there something about God you learned from your father? Your mother? I have found even those who came from nonreligious backgrounds still learned something of God's character from each of their parents.

Second, honoring your parents allows them to remain connected to your children. I'm concerned with the way many grandparents are becoming isolated from their families. Why is it so many older people are so bored? Why are they under-challenged? What keeps them going as they approach the end of life? Why do so many waste so much time chasing little white balls around a golf course? Why are they so nonchalant about their grandchildren, their legacy? Here they are at the end of their lives, and most don't have any compelling vision to focus on, let alone pass on to the next generation.

Something tells me the problem in many cases may be their relationship with their adult children. If you were to say to me, "I wish my parents would start making time to be grandparents," I would ask, "How much time are you spending with your parents?" Or, "How are you, practically speaking, pursuing a relationship with them?" Perhaps if we value the older generation by honoring our parents, they will value the younger generation by getting involved in their grandchildren's lives.

Your children are watching you and will follow your model.

Do they feel close to you? Do they feel loved, appreciated, and needed? And if they are needed, is it for something other than just babysitting? If they did, perhaps they would make the effort to be involved.

God gives grandparents a special role in a child's life. A child may learn some character qualities from his grandparents more than from his parents. That's the type of vision I'd like to give grandparents: help build another generation.

I realize not all grandparents will be able to do this. I also realize your parents make their own choices. Even if you do fulfill your responsibility to honor them, they may not take on the role you'd like them to. Even so, by honoring them you are making an attempt to connect your kids to the family legacy.

Third, honoring your parents may result in your children honoring you.

Do you want your children to regard you as wise when you are older? Do you want them to listen to you when you're as old as your parents are now? Your children are watching you and will follow your model. If you aren't honoring your parents, then you run the risk of having your children treat you in the same way.

A friend was sitting on his sofa one night when his wife said with a sigh, "I guess it's time to go call my mother." Then she stopped, looked at her oldest daughter, and said, "I guess twenty years from now Amy will probably be saying that while sitting on the sofa with her husband." That's when she realized she was teaching her daughter to dishonor her.

The Legacy of a Slave

When you honor your parents and teach your children to do the same, you allow a spiritual legacy to pass from one generation to the next.

Let me tell you about Peter Loritts, a man most would never have considered successful, but who is having an impact on our culture today.

Peter began his life as a slave in North Carolina. Released after President Lincoln's Emancipation Proclamation, he eventually acquired some farmland. He never learned to read or write.

Two things were important to Peter. First, he loved the Lord. His niece Vera remembered him as a "singing and praying man." He often had his children and grandchildren read him passages from the Bible, which he committed to memory. When his church needed land for a building, he donated part of his farm.

He also was committed to his family. He provided for them and raised them to love the Lord. He passed on to them a heritage of honesty and integrity and strong male leadership.

Peter's son, Crawford, was like his father in many ways. He believed in commitment and responsibility. If he promised something, he'd do it. He used to tell his children to "never walk away from responsibility. You look it in its eye and you deal with it, but you don't just walk away."

When Crawford's son, Crawford Jr., wanted to quit a job he had just begun, his dad asked why. "I just don't like it there anymore, Dad," he replied.

"Son, you gave the man your word that you'd show up. Not liking something is no reason to quit. Your word is everything. You said you'd be there, so you are not going to quit."

Crawford, the son of a slave, grew up in the rural south in the heyday of the Ku Klux Klan. He faced the same discrimination many other black men faced. But he never allowed his children to use race for an excuse. "Throughout life he would remind us to rise above that, to look beyond that," Crawford Jr. recalls. "And he would refuse to typify white people as all being the same. He had a number of white friends he worked with. And he would bring us in contact with models of people who loved us for who we were, and always point out the differences, and he would give us tongue lashings if we ever generalized all white people."

"There are three men in my life who mean a lot to me: the Lord Jesus, my grandfather for what he stands for, and my dad. I want to be like those three."

Crawford Jr. grew up to attend a Bible college and became a minister. Today he is pastor of a church in Roswell, Georgia, is one of the most popular speakers for our Weekend to Remember® marriage getaways, and has served on the board of directors for several organizations, including FamilyLife. Most important, he is a husband, a father, and a grandfather. He passed on to his four children the same lessons he learned from his father that his father had learned from his father.

"It's funny how you catch yourself saying the same things that your dad said to you," he said. When his boys were in sports, he would tell them, "If you play, you stay. I don't want to hear any nonsense about you quitting because you don't like it or because the coach yelled at you."

Before his father died, Crawford Jr. and Karen would take the children up to the old homestead in Conover, North Carolina, to visit him. "They loved to sit on the porch with their grandfather and he would tell stories," Crawford said. "The sense of connectedness and destiny that gave them is absolutely incredible."

Peter Loritts had no grand scheme for passing on godly character from one generation to another, but that's what happened. And it continues. Crawford Jr.'s oldest son, Bryan, is a pastor and speaker. At one conference, Bryan introduced his dad by saying, "There are three men in my life who mean a lot to me: the Lord Jesus, my grandfather for what he stands for, and my dad. I want to be like those three."

That's the power of legacy—the connection from one generation to the next, and to the next, and to the next. And honor is what makes it possible.

Bryan Loritts's Tribute to His Father

I had the privilege of mentoring Bryan Loritts for several years, and during that time I encouraged him to write a tribute to his father. He had an opportunity to present it when a number of us surprised Crawford with a banquet honoring him for his life and ministry. At the end of the evening, Bryan went to the podium and read the following tribute to Crawford in front of 250 friends.

> I recently came home from a busy weekend of ministry to discover that my younger son, Myles, had learned to walk while I was away. My heart was gripped as never before at the realization that I had missed a significant moment in his life. I had to fight back tears as I wrestled with whether or not I had failed him in some way. And so late that night, I quietly slipped out of bed and into his room, peeking down at him while he was fast asleep in his crib.

As I laid my hands on him to pray, I wondered if there would be other moments, significant ones, that I would miss in his life. As never before, I felt the sometimes conflicting paths of pastoral ministry and family. While under this burden that night my thoughts were on you, Dad. Since then I've pondered one particular question: How did you bear such a burden so well?

As my mind has contemplated this question over the past months, several specific things you did have come to my mind. I remember as a little boy, when Atlanta got its annual half-inch of snow, the whole city made its way to Kroger to buy milk and bread, thinking that we would all die. I was mad at you for being gone; that is, until you called. When Mom handed me the phone, you asked me what I thought you should do. I said, "Come home, Dad." You told me you were canceling your meetings to come home early . . . and sure enough, you were there.

I remember all those times we fished on the bank of some Georgia lake or pond. I laugh now as I think of the distinguished, world-renowned Crawford Loritts struggling to put a night crawler on a hook. But that's just it. When I was growing up, while everyone looked at you as some celebrity, I just saw you as Dad, helping me catch bream or catfish.

You taught me the importance of integrity. You would tell me over and over again that when I told someone I was going to do something, to do it—after all, that's what Loritts men do. You never once made a promise to me you didn't keep. While as a child I expected to see you at my ballgames (many times still in your coat and tie), as a father now I see the sacrifice you made to keep your promise and to be there. Thanks, Dad. I even remember bragging that the cashier lady at Dairy Queen gave me a dime too much in change once. You quickly turned me around and told me to go back in and give her the dime—yet another lesson in integrity.

How you treated my mother continues to be a profound lesson in my marriage to Korie. I never once heard you raise your voice at Mom. I never saw you talk to her in a condescending way, but only in a manner that communicated the utmost respect. While divorce was the norm among my friends' parents, I never even contemplated that scenario in our home. In fact, the only time I really feared your lashing out in anger at someone was when a man in our neighborhood cursed my mother in your presence. I can still hear you say to that man, "Sir, I love Jesus, but I swear, if you come across this street, I will whup your behind."

Something tells me that, more than anything, Dad, your incredible love for Christ is what allowed you to lead your family so well. One of my earliest childhood recollections is running in on you early in the morning as you were on your knees in prayer before God. Times around the dinner table as you opened the Scriptures were where God formed in me a passion for Him and His Word. When I acknowledged this call into ministry and went off to Bible college, I can still hear your final words ringing in my ears as you prepared to leave: "Son, obey God." Dad, I'm trying.

Dad, I want to thank you for one more thing. Thank you for giving me a name that I can wear with pride. You've kept the name Loritts free from scandal, and dripping with moral purity. Wherever I am in this country, people know that name and they respect it—and it's because of your obedience to God and commitment to integrity.

The late E. K. Bailey would give me a hundred dollars every time I saw him because of that name. Tony Evans and Bishop Eddie Long gave me jobs because of that name. Bishop Kenneth Ulmer has mentored and fathered me because of that name. Dennis and Barbara Rainey have profoundly influenced my wife and me because of that name. And in many regards it's that name that helps to put food on the table in my home today.

Your life has given me an incredible challenge—to live in such a way that my wife and kids can wear the name Loritts with pride as well. And by God's grace I will.

I love you,
Bryan

Bryan struggled to read the tribute that night because of his emotions. When he finished Crawford got up and they wept in each other's arms.

"The next day my father told me that he couldn't sleep that night and read my tribute again and cried some more," Bryan wrote soon after. "His exact words were, 'You have no idea how much those words mean to me.' "

Bryan then put into words what many adult children feel when they honor their parents in a significant way. "I feel like my soul exhaled. It's like I was carrying this burden around with me that I didn't know about as it relates to my dad, and now it's gone . . . We've instantly gone to another level."

5 WAYS TO HONOR YOUR PARENTS BY KEEPING THE FAMILY LEGACY ALIVE

1. **Encourage your parents to tell your children stories about the past.** People love to talk about the past, and children often love hearing the old stories. It gives them a connection with their parents and grandparents.

2. Develop an audio or video history of your family by interviewing your parents, grandparents, and other relatives. Family stories will disappear unless you record them. If you capture them before a parent dies, those recordings will become some of your most cherished possessions.

3. Organize old family photos and produce books for the family. You and your parents may have boxes of old photos. Go through them and choose the best. Scan photos into your computer, and then use an online service to create photo books for your parents' birthdays, anniversaries, etc.

4. Transfer old home movies onto DVDs and give copies to each family member for Christmas. Better yet, edit the movies before transferring them to highlight the best sections.

5. Revisit their childhood homes. Most parents love to return to their old neighborhoods. I once drove with my mom and my daughter, Ashley, to look at Mom's old homestead. The house was abandoned and taken over by cows. We walked inside and talked about what life was like there. She remembered where they used to slaughter hogs and render the lard, and how they made cracklins. We talked about where the barn used to be and how she gathered eggs as a little girl. We talked about what her mom and dad were like, and the golden anniversary they celebrated just a few short years before both of them died. Mom enjoyed the trip, and it was a great way for Ashley to catch a glimpse of her heritage.

father do? Rather than punishing the son, he restores him to a full relationship.

A Modern-Day Prodigal

One woman who wrote me knew what it means to have a prodigal child. Her oldest daughter, Anne, was a problem child at an early age. "From age two she was a very 'anti'-personality," the mother wrote. "She disliked what everyone else liked. She enjoyed what others disliked."

When Anne was a third grader, her parents took her to see a professional counselor. He described her behavior as that of a typical rebellious teenager, and she was just eight years old! "There were many prayers and many tears for many years. At various low points in her life we took her for counseling, but it usually ended with her feeling resentful, angry, and worthless, her mother recalls.

When Anne was in her twenties, she agreed to see a Christian counselor with her parents. After several years of visits the wall was broken down.

Anne eventually became a wife and mother herself. And one year she presented her mother with this tribute on Mother's Day:

A TRIBUTE TO MY MOTHER

whom I hated for many years
her graying head hung down
hurt and sadness in her eyes
knees bent beside her bed, hands
and fingers clenched in prayer,
rejection and bitterness causing her despair.
I had, through walls of anger and resentment,

withheld my love from her
because I thought she didn't care.
And yet she did care and took that
all important step,
she asked me to go with her.
Together she and I surged ahead
in sorrow and joy
through years of sharing and counseling.
Forgiving each other and forgetting the past
we learned to accept each other
for who we are,
mother and daughter,
and friends.

Can you imagine how this mother felt when Anne finally expressed her gratitude? She had waited for years for Anne to grow out of her rebellion, and then several more for her daughter to experience motherhood herself. And finally she heard the words she had longed to hear.

Whether you were a prodigal child or enjoyed a good relationship with your parents, the question you should ask is, Are they waiting? It is time to start building a road back home. It is time to give your parents what they need—honor and a relationship with you. If you give it, you will benefit beyond measure. You have God's word on it.

With all these benefits available, you'd think it would be easy for us to honor our parents. But many of us—*most* of us—still don't honor them, do we?

Thank You to Mama

Many years ago, Bill Barber felt tension in his relationship with his mother. "We weren't getting along too well," he said. "When I was young, we were always pulling pranks on each other." As they aged, that was no longer the case.

After he read my book *The Tribute,* he decided to honor his mother with a written tribute. He chose to keep it simple. Apparently it made an impression. In the years before his mother died, she lost her ability to speak, but not to point. Whenever a visitor came to her bedside, she pointed to the tribute that hung over her bed.

Here is what her visitors read:

Dear Mama,

Thank you for having me. I know you weren't supposed to—medically speaking—but you did anyway. And thank you for putting up with me as a little kid. And thank you for not throwing me away 'cause I blacked your little dolls' faces. And thanks for staying up all night with me when I had the measles and chills and fever, and hugging me all night. And thank you for staying with me in the Scott and White Hospital when I had my knee operation. And thank you for not killing me when you caught me pouring the medicine down the sink (when I was anemic).

And thank you for taking me on a picnic one time across the river. And thank you for taking me to the air base when you worked out there. And thank you for getting me elected as "king" of the high school. And thank you for nursing me and getting me on that bus to go play in that All-Star game. And thank you for washing my clothes, especially in college. And thank you for taking me to Glosserman's and getting me a new suit to wear to the homecoming dance, and thank you for understanding about my many girlfriends.

And thank you for nursing me when I passed out in front of Joske's while you were buying Charlotte's wedding dress. And thank you for visiting me in the hospital when I had a wreck and I was so bored I flipped boogers on the ceiling.

And thank you for understanding me when I played post office [an old kissing game] and told about it. And thank you for the time you put salt in the sugar bowl on April Fool's Day. And thank you for understanding when I wouldn't wear a tie to Charlotte's wedding.

And thank you for coming to stay with us when we had Clay and Bob. And thank you for coming to stay with us when Jean had rheumatic fever and then rheumatoid arthritis, and then when Bob had his finger operated on.

And thank you for always just forgiving me and Jean and our boys for all [of our] faults and sins and overlooking things. And thank you for laughing at the world no matter what, 'cause I learned it too, and I have you to thank. Amen.

With love,
Your son, Bill

(8)

THE GIFT OF UNDERSTANDING

Christians are like school children who like to look at the back of the book for the answers rather than go through the process.

—Søren Kierkegaard

Dan Jarrell's father died when he was fifteen, leaving Dan's mother with three teenagers to raise alone. The kids did not process their dad's death very well. In fact, at times this single mom saw her family teeter on the edge of disaster.

Spiritually, Dan was dead. If God would take his dad, then Dan wanted no part of Him. So this angry teenager rebelled.

Dan turned to drugs and alcohol to fill the father-shaped void in his life. At eighteen, he was arrested for criminal activity in narcotics. While serving probation, Dan continued to ignore his mom's pleas to change his ways. At six foot three and two hundred forty pounds, he was big enough to intimidate her, and he refused to submit to her authority.

At twenty-two years of age Dan became a Christian. As God became increasingly real to him, he began to shed the baggage of anger he had carried for years. His attitude toward his mom began to change, but unfortunately the relationship grew distant. Later he began to understand why. When he had told his mom about his spiritual rebirth, she'd seen it as a rejection of all he had learned growing up in their church.

The strain grew for more than a decade until Dan decided to write and present a tribute to his mother. "It was a watershed in our relationship," Dan told me.

As Dan worked on his tribute, he sought to understand his mom. As he reflected on the memories, both good and bad, he began to realize the price she had paid in raising three children after the sudden death of her husband. Now a father himself, Dan weighed the struggles he was experiencing as a father. The more he reflected, the more she seemed a heroine than an adversary.

Understanding Is the Key

I'll finish Dan's story at the end of this chapter, but note that he began to bridge the gulf between himself and his mother when he sought to understand her. As self-absorbed children, we analyze our parents for our own selfish purposes. We know a lot about them, but we've never sought to understand them.

We know a lot about them, but we've never sought to understand them.

In order to honor your parents, it's important for you to give them three gifts: understanding, compassion, and forgiveness.

I begin with the gift of understanding because many people have found it to be the key to unlocking their ability to honor their parents. Proverbs 24:3–4 tells us, "By wisdom a house is built, and by understanding it is established; by knowledge the rooms are filled with all precious and pleasant riches." If you have difficulty relating to your parents, or if your parents have hurt you in some way, you may need to step back and look at them in a fresh way as people. By looking at your parents more objectively, by seeing them through the eyes of Christ, you may be able to understand more clearly why your problems are occurring.

Focusing on the Flaws

As we move through our teenage years and into adulthood, most of us begin to see our parents as human beings with their own unique weaknesses and blemishes. And because of our natural bent toward the negative, we find it easy to focus on the mistakes they made. It is often here that many adult children make the wrong choice. Rather than seeking to understand and honor their parents, they judge and condemn them.

Understanding our parents will move us from rejecting them for their mistakes toward honoring them for what they did right. When we see them as people with needs, we are compelled as their children to reach out and give back a portion of the love they have attempted to give us.

"The Pedestal of Our Imaginations"

In an article in *Christian Century* magazine, J. Wesley Brown urged adult children to take a realistic view of their parents.

> Honor your father and mother. Negatively, it means not to confuse parents with God in your life. Positively, it means to accept them as they are—human beings, frail creatures whom God loves no less than God loves little children. And when parents get to be 60 or 70 years old, they have not ceased to be God's children. That they did not have total wisdom when they raised

> us, that they did not always know exactly what to tell us, what to let us do and what to prevent us from doing, does not mean they did not love us and intend to do well by us . . .
>
> Perhaps the greatest honor we can do our parents is to let them down off the pedestal of our imaginations, where we are inclined either to idolize them or to flog them as gods who failed (as indeed they must fail), and to accept them as people—people who need forgiveness as well as respect, who need honest relationships with their children perhaps more than with anyone else.[1]

Something happened inside of me when I realized two things. First, much of what I had longed for and expected from my parents were needs that could be met only by God. Second, my parents were human beings with needs, just like me. That's when I took my parents off the pedestal and decided to let them be human. Soon I began to understand them as people with hurts and struggles of their own, and a deep need for love.

In order to begin the process of understanding your parents, I have three suggestions:

Step One: Look at Your Parents' Needs

When you look at your mother, what do you see? A sixty-year-old woman who still seems to treat you like a child? Or do you picture her as a twenty-five-year-old, striving to earn the approval of her own mother? Do you see her as a woman trying to keep her marriage together? Or do you see her as a cranky, elderly woman whose body is starting to fall apart and who doesn't know how to cope emotionally?

When you look at your father, what do you see? A successful businessman who spent too little time with you and your siblings? Or a lonely, insecure man who had so many holes in his life created by his parents that the only way he knew to cope was by working harder, longer hours? Do you see him as a man who has never said, "I love you," or as an eight-year-old boy, continually criticized by his father? At the end of his life, do you think he feels successful in what really matters, or is he haunted by his poor choices and wrong values?

Take a fresh look at your parents. Sometimes it is easy to forget that within a parent beats the heart of a small child, a teenager, a parent, and a frightened and helpless human being who desperately needs love and care.

The following poem makes a powerful statement about understanding what lies beneath the surface of an elderly parent.

Look Closer

What do you see, nurse, what do you see,
What do you think of when you look at me?
A crabbed old woman, not very wise
Uncertain of habit, with faraway eyes.
Who dribbles her food and makes no reply
When you say in a loud voice, "I do wish you'd try."

Who seems not to notice the things that you do
And forever is losing a stocking or shoe.
Who, unresisting or not, lets you do as you will
With bathing and feeding, the long day to fill.
Is that what you're thinking, is that what you see?
Then open your eyes, you're not looking at me.

I'll tell you who I am as I sit here so still,
As I move at your bidding, as I eat at your will.
I'm a small child of ten with a father and mother,
Brothers and sisters who love one another.

A young girl at sixteen with wings on her feet
Dreaming that soon now a lover she'll meet.
A bride soon at twenty . . . my heart gives a leap
Remembering the vows that I promised to keep.

At twenty-five now I have young of my own
Who need me to build a secure happy home.
A woman of thirty, my young now grow fast,
Bound to each other with ties that should last.

At forty my young now will soon be gone
But my man stays beside me to see I don't mourn.
At fifty once more babies play round my knee
Again we know children, my loved one and me.

Dark days are upon me, my husband is dead.
I look at the future and shudder with dread.
For my young are all busy rearing young of their own.
And I think of the years and the love I have known.

I'm an old lady now and nature is cruel.
'Tis her jest to make old age look like a fool.
The body it crumbles, grace and vigor depart,
And now there's a stone where I once had a heart.

But inside this old carcass a young girl still dwells
And now and again my battered heart swells.
I remember the joys, I remember the pain
And I'm loving and living life over again.
I think of the years all too few—gone so fast
And accept the stark fact that nothing can last.
So open your eyes, nurses, open and see
Not a crabbed old woman, look closer—see me.[2]

—Phyllis McCormack

Step Two: Learn More About Their Background

I suggest you take a step back, take off the title of daughter or son, and take a brief but realistic inventory of your mom and dad:

- How did they get to this point in their lives?
- What events, circumstances, and choices made them who they have become?
- What did they have to overcome to achieve what they accomplished?
- What were their major disappointments in life?
- What kind of families did they grow up in?
- How were they treated by their mom and dad?

Take off the glasses they smudged due to mistakes they made in your childhood and ask God to give you clear vision, a new perspective of your mom and dad. Take time to talk to your parents, to get to know them as people. Over a period of time, ask them questions about their family background. Begin working on a family history and interview them about their experiences. Ask them why they made the choices they made. Probe them with questions that will force them to reveal more of who they are.

Take time to talk to your parents, to get to know them as people.

If your grandparents are alive, look closely at your parents' relationship with them. You might find that your parents experienced many of the same frustrations that you do.

A young woman told me about her shallow relationship with her domineering mother. Then she mentioned her grandmother. "Every time I see my grandmother, it reminds me why my mom is the way she is. Mom feels her mom is critical. They relate to each other, but they don't ever relate about feelings."

A careful inventory of their background will enlarge your heart and perspective to better understand your parents.

Step Three: Get in Their Shoes

If you are disappointed in how your parents raised you, try to imagine the struggles and pressures they must have felt at that time—economic pressures, social pressures, health struggles, problems with extended family, emotional struggles, just to name a few possibilities. Maybe they experienced a business failure, an unexpected financial setback, or some significant life-altering circumstance.

If you have children of your own, think of your parents experiencing some of the same pressures you are working through right now—toddlers and teenagers constantly pressing the limits, helping a child cope with peer pressure, the onslaught of adolescent hormones and emotions . . .

Many adults complain that their parents continue to treat them like children. If you have children, think of how you relate to your kids now, and then visualize how difficult it will be to let them go and relate to them differently. Imagine a professional tennis player who spends twenty years honing his craft. Then you approach him and say, "It's time for you to give up that skill. You're now going to play golf. And by the way, I've entered you in a tournament next week." That's how difficult it can be for parents. They spend years developing skills and habits in parenting, then all the rules change once their birds leave the nest. They may have never been told they needed to be working toward the day when the nature of this relationship was going to change.

Step Four: Reflect back and capture a memory of when your parents did something right

Many adults find it difficult to achieve a proper balance in how they view their parents; they don't want to let go of a negative, critical view.

Sometimes it's easier to maintain the victim mindset that says, "They blew it, and I'm paying the price! I'm the one who is messed up. I'm the one who's having a problem in my marriage. I'm the one who gets angry with these kids."

In reality, most parents did the best they could with what little wisdom they had. But they make the mistakes that have plagued the human race since the beginning of time.

I could judge my father harshly for some of his weaknesses and mistakes. I don't recall seeing my dad pray apart from special thanksgivings offered before supper and occasionally at church. He was a very private man. He made his fair share of mistakes, too. I remember a quarrel with Mom when he never did admit he was wrong. He brought home a car he bought for my brother and me, all without consulting my mom. Having been a husband for years, I now have my own list of errors like that to compare with his.

Maybe he worked too much building his own business. He probably watched too much television on the weekends. He was too strict on my brother and too lenient with me. He should have asked me a lot more questions about where I was going and where I had been. But, all things considered, Dad was very effective as a father; he was a winner. As a boy, I would measure him and our family with what my friends experienced. I always liked my dad and my home best.

In reality, most parents did the best they could.

I always knew he loved me. The scrapbook he kept secretly of my athletic career through high school and college told me that. Dad taught me character and integrity. He showed me how to be a winner and compete fairly as he coached my Little League team. He lived responsibly. He had difficulty getting a credit card in the late 1960s because he had no credit references; he had always paid cash and never borrowed any money.

He left me with a thousand vivid memories of playing catch; of three Canadian fishing trips; of hunting for rabbit, deer, and quail;

of skipping rocks, of teaching me how to drive (I sat on his lap while driving down a deserted gravel road), and of visiting and caring for his mom—all the things that feed a relationship and make it thrive.

Even today, I look back at what my dad did right and wrong. If I wanted to, I could focus on his deficits and errors. I imagine I have some flaws in my character because Dad did not raise me as well as he might have. Yet, because I seek to honor my dad I have not spent much time focusing on his shortcomings. You see, I now understand his roots. In fact, the older I become, the more amazed I am that Dad turned out to be the man of character that he was.

Dad grew up in a log cabin with seven brothers and sisters. His father deserted the family when Dad was a teenager. Dad helped raise his brothers and sisters and trapped wild animals to help put food on the table. All of this provides an even greater appreciation for what he did right. He raised his family in an age when fathers were expected to be providers more than communicators. And yet he did his best to communicate with me, at his level. He was involved in my life.

I believe there comes a point when every son or daughter needs to consciously lay aside the mistakes of their parents and focus on what they did right. Just as I did with my dad.

Appreciating the Good Things She Did

You can tell when you are beginning to understand your parents. Their behavior toward you may not change, but you will find you don't react the same. You will find it is easier to give them grace because you view them differently.

That's what happened with Dan Jarrell when he began working on a tribute to his mother. Putting himself in her shoes helped him appreciate the good things she had done in raising him.

Writing her tribute took time and care. His final product was a tribute full of praise and respect for the hard choices she had to make to raise three teenagers. It focused on her strengths.

Here is Dan's tribute to his mother, Dorothy Jarrell.

To Mom,

I respect you, Mother, for the courage it takes to get up and keep living when everything in your world falls apart. Few women left alone with three teenagers to raise could face that reality with the steadfast determination you have shown. With wisdom beyond your experience you refused to control me. You had the courage to let me fail and then to help me face the wages of my own choices. From you I learned that courage and confidence are not the same thing. Courage is a commitment to do what is right even when you have no confidence at all. I saw such courage in my father, but I learned it from you.

I honor you, Mother, for the strength it takes to deny your own needs for the sake of those who need you. Strength to be both mom and dad to a hard-headed boy who thinks he's a man. Strength to work full time in the marketplace and yet never let home be a second priority. Every morning of my life I woke up to breakfast before school. Every time I needed you, you were there. You said no to me, knowing I would fight you. You challenged me when I was certain to argue and confronted me when you knew I would defend myself and accuse you of being unfair. From you I learned that strength is usually a silent virtue. Strength quietly sacrifices for the sake of higher good. It never expects honor and seldom receives it. You have shown me what it really means to be strong, and it has marked my life.

I praise you, Mother! You were faithful when many would have given up. You were flexible when many would refuse to grow and change. You were fun even in the midst of some painful times for our family. The quality of my life and the substance of my character are largely of your making. The sacrifices you made to invest in me will impact my children and my children's children. For all that you are and all you have done . . .

. . . I love you, Mom!

Dan did it right. He typeset the tribute on parchment, matted and framed it, and called his mom to tell her he was coming home. He did not tell her why.

He left his wife and kids at home to spend six days on the coast of Oregon laughing, playing, and fishing with his mom—the things she liked to do. On the last evening Dan took her out to eat at a nice restaurant. Then they returned to her hotel room and Dan gave her the tribute. Sitting by her side on the bed, Dan read it to her.

Recounting the emotions of the moment caused Dan to cry as he told me the story. "She just sat there on the edge of the bed weeping and hugging the tribute like it was a baby."

Dan gave his mom the tribute she deserved, but it was his gift of understanding that reconnected his heart to hers. It wasn't until he became a parent himself that he truly comprehended the hardships she had faced and the heartaches he had given her as a son.

"She wondered if I really believed some of the wonderful comments I made about her," Dan told me. "It wasn't flattery; it was the truth."

(9)

THE GIFT OF COMPASSION

Once an adult. Twice a child.

—A GRANDFATHER'S PROVERB

I was watching the Olympic Games one evening when I observed a scene of compassion I will never forget. Derek Redmond of Great Britain was running a 400-meter semifinal when he fell to the track with a hamstring injury. But to the crowd's surprise, he got up and began hobbling around the track, trying to finish his race.

Then suddenly a man jumped from the grandstands onto the track. That man was Derek's father, Jim, who had just watched his son's Olympic dream fall apart. And he knew what he needed to do. "I was thinking I had to get him there so he could say he finished the semifinal," Jim Redmond said.

Jim reached Derek's side and took his arm. When Derek saw who it was, he began sobbing. And together, arm-in-arm, they finished the race to the cheers of the crowd.[1]

This is a great picture of a parent showing compassion for a child. And in a way it is symbolic of situations we all find ourselves in as we go through life. There are times when parents need to support their children as they pursue their goals. And later in life those children need to hold up their parents as they approach the finish line. I have come to see that many adults need to show the same type of compassion toward their parents that they received as children.

Feeling Accompanied by Action

Compassion is love in action. If understanding involves looking at your parents through the eyes of Christ, then compassion involves responding to your parents with the heart of Christ.

Understanding our parents should lead us to "put on . . . compassionate hearts" (Colossians 3:12) and then take specific steps to demonstrate that compassion to them. Biblical compassion always results in action.

The gospel of Matthew records several telling examples of Jesus Christ's compassion. Matthew 9:35–36 describes how Jesus visited cities and villages "teaching in their synagogues and proclaiming the gospel of the kingdom and healing every disease and every affliction. When he saw the crowds, he had compassion for them, because they were harassed and helpless, like sheep without a shepherd." Jesus understood the spiritual and emotional condition of the people. And He took action as a result. Matthew 14:14 notes, "When he went ashore he saw a great crowd, and he had compassion on them and healed their sick."

Compassion involves responding to your parents with the heart of Christ.

Matthew 20:29–34 describes an encounter Jesus had with two blind men. "They said to him, 'Lord, let our eyes be opened.' And Jesus in pity touched their eyes, and immediately they recovered their sight and followed him."

And Matthew 15:32 records how Jesus told the disciples, "I have compassion on the crowd because they have been with me now three days and have nothing to eat. And I am unwilling to send them away hungry, lest they faint on the way."

In each case, Jesus' feelings of compassion developed from seeing and understanding their circumstances. And then this compassion led Him to take steps to help.

Three Reasons for Being Compassionate Toward Parents

To help us to "put on compassionate hearts" toward our parents, we need to look at them from a different vantage point. Let me suggest three reasons why adult children should have compassion on parents.

First, parents need compassion because raising children is an exhausting and painful process. And 99 percent of the energy given to the process will never be remembered by our children.

Did your parents ever say something like this to you: "I sure hope if you get married and have kids God gives you one just like you"? My mom did, while I was a teenager of less than model behavior. She always made it clear she loved me and thought it was a privilege to be my mom. But she was also sending me a message: You'll never know the challenges, the worry you caused me, and the emotional stretch I went through to be your mom. And just so that you feel some of it I hope you get at least one child like you!

Her prayers were answered, numerous times. We have six children and I won't tell you how many are like me.

Second, some parents need compassion because their children have brought deep pain to their lives. I have watched parents age at an accelerated rate when dealing with a rebellious child. The child has rejected them, their values, and is doing his or her best to hurt the parents.

In an interview on *FamilyLife Today®*, author and speaker Josh McDowell told of his older brother's rebellion against his parents and how it affected his mother. "I came home from a date when I was a senior in high school and Mom was crying. Weeping. I asked her, 'What's wrong?' She said, 'Your father and your brother have broken my heart, and all I want to do is live until you graduate. Then I just want to die.' "

Two months later Josh graduated; his mother died two weeks later. "I blamed my brother," Josh commented. "Mom died of a broken heart."

Third, parents need compassion because as they grow older they increasingly experience loss. They just cannot do what they used to do. Losses due to aging come in all kinds of shapes and sizes, resulting in significant adjustments. They may suffer physical losses, like their good health, physical strength, stamina, hearing, or eyesight. They may lose family members or friends. And many may lose their sense of purpose. Your parents may grieve over their limitations. They may become angry over their aging. They need your compassion, your friendship, to ease the pain of these losses.

The final years of a parent's life constitute a terrible and wonderful irony. On one hand, you have an adult full of experience and wisdom, once strong and vibrant, now helplessly feeling trapped while watching his body deteriorate. With each passing year, he becomes more dependent upon others. If he lives long enough, he may become totally unable to care for himself.

Giving Your Time

Real compassion may extract a sacrifice. That's why it's so valuable. The sacrifice will involve giving your time—time to help out and time to talk and listen and love without an agenda.

My dad modeled this beautifully with his own mother. I recall as a boy going with him to her house after dinner. We'd sit in our chairs, sometimes talking and sometimes not. I remember how impatient I would become when nobody said anything. The only sounds were the tick of an old cuckoo clock and the creak in Grandma's rocking chair.

I realize now that Dad was being compassionate. One of my problems is I'm an active person, and when I used to go visit my mom, I'd have real problems sitting still. Over time, I got the point . . . she needed me to come visit and just be there with her.

Real compassion may extract a sacrifice.

What are your parents' needs right now? Emotional? Spiritual? Physical? Taking them to the doctor? Repairing a dripping faucet or mowing their lawn? Or taking a walk with one of them? Perhaps it's as simple as a letter or as complex as bringing them into your home during the final years of their lives.

The needs of aging parents can change, and we need to be available to them and continually be good students of what they need just like they tried to do with us when we were children.

Meeting Spiritual Needs

Perhaps you are rightly concerned with the spiritual needs of your parents and want to do all you can to reach out and help them. It could be that writing a tribute may not only bust a logjam in your relationship but, perhaps, open the stream of communication to discuss their relationship with God.

It all begins with prayer. Ask God to soften their hearts to receive and feel the words of love in your tribute. Pray for an opportunity to share God's love and forgiveness that is found in His son Jesus Christ.

Over the past four decades I've counseled hundreds of adult children and one thing has become very clear: It is very difficult for parents to receive spiritual direction from their children. Perhaps this is due to pride, or maybe they know us too well. So go slow with your parents. Be careful about shoving Christianity down their throats. Many have tried and failed, paying the price for their insensitivity for years.

At the right time and in the right place, God can move in unusual ways to give you the opportunity to engage your parents and help them consider their spiritual needs. I know of a son who found God's forgiveness through Jesus Christ, and then began praying for his father, a drunkard who had abused him for much of his life. Then the son was critically injured in an automobile accident.

The father visited his son, who was near death. There in the hospital the son said he wanted to forgive him for all his father had done to him. The father broke and began to weep, asking, "How can you forgive me for all I've done to you?"

That opened the door for the son to share with him how he had recently found God's forgiveness through His son Jesus Christ. The father became a Christian later that day.

Someday you may find yourself in a similar situation, suddenly reaching out to your parent and seeking to meet his needs. Eventually these individuals, once so strong and independent, will find themselves limping rather than running the race of life. Could it be they will need you to come out of the stands and onto the track to help them finish the race?

(10)

THE GIFT OF FORGIVENESS

Children begin by loving their parents. After a time, they judge them. Rarely, if ever, do they forgive them.
—Oscar Wilde

Many of you will find that seeking to understand your parents and have compassion for them will lead inevitably to the final gift you should give them—forgiveness.

One writer told of her father, who was a domineering man who had ruled his household harshly. After she grew into an adult and became a Christian she observed, "God allowed me to see my earthly father as a boy in an aging body; a boy who, like most of us, wants his own way. Once I saw beneath his facade, I realized that I might not have liked his actions, but that I truly loved him. To my joy and amazement, that revelation enabled me to forgive him."[1]

For many adult children, forgiveness is the most difficult gift. When they think of their parents, they are unable to break free from the hurt and pain of the past. Mentally and verbally they rehash and rehearse old hurts like a song stuck on replay.

In reality some parents are guilty; their actions and mistakes are indefensible. Parents are responsible for their failures and certainly for any evil abuse. But at some point we've got to emotionally stop prosecuting them for their mistakes.

A failure to forgive and seek forgiveness results in an angry heart, resentment, and bitterness.

A failure to forgive and seek forgiveness results in an angry heart, resentment, and bitterness. Left to run their course, unrestrained, these emotions will destroy a relationship. But forgiveness makes reconciliation and restoration possible. Forgiveness makes long-term relationships possible.

A Terrible Tragedy

It was a mistake any five-year-old child could make. Nonetheless, it was childish disobedience that resulted in a tragedy. A triple tragedy.

Cindy loved being with her younger brother Andy, who was two. They were buddies. They played together, ate together, and enjoyed dressing up together. So when their mom left them alone at the house for a few minutes to run an errand, it was only natural that Cindy, the ringleader, should seize the moment.

She knew it was wrong. She had been warned never to do it. But she did it anyway. Cindy played with the matches.

The house caught fire and burned down.

Cindy escaped. Andy didn't.

After the fire, Cindy's mother just couldn't look at her daughter without being reminded of what she had done. The pain in her mother's heart grew so intense that one day she announced to Cindy, "I don't want you anymore. It is just too painful. Every time I look at you I'm reminded of your horrible mistake."

So, she gave Cindy up for adoption and moved away, refusing to ever see her daughter again.

Cindy's aunt intervened and took her in, adopting her and raising her. This aunt led Cindy to faith in Christ at a young age.

Through the years Cindy's faith deepened, although her struggles through the teenage years were intense. As she grew into adulthood, she had to confront her feelings about her mother. Yes, Cindy had made a terrible mistake, but how could her mother have disowned her?

Cindy realized she couldn't continue to harbor bitterness in her heart. So she chose to forgive her mother.

When Cindy turned thirty, she sought out her mother and asked if she would meet with her, just once. She wanted to show her mom she had turned out all right, that she was a good Christian woman, leading a productive life. And indeed she was, for she had become a woman with a countenance of peace that never revealed her deep hurt.

To her surprise, her mother accepted the invitation to meet for dinner. Cindy was thrilled and hopeful; it had been twenty-five years.

Finally the day came. Cindy cautiously opened up about her life as they ate their meal. But her mother's growing silence was a signal that all was not well. At the end of the meal, she told Cindy that seeing her brought back all those terrible memories. She asked her never to contact her again.

We Hurt Them, They Hurt Us

Hurt, disappointment, pain—it's the nature of relationships. We fail one another. Punish each other. Our parents damage us and we injure them. That's the tragedy of what Cindy and her mom experienced.

But they dealt with it differently. By forgiving her mother, Cindy felt free to attempt to reconcile with her. She had peace. But by choosing not to forgive Cindy, her mother exiled her daughter and committed herself to a path eroded by anger and bitterness.

Many of you may find that forgiving your parents is the most critical step you need to take to establish a new relationship with them. It may be the only thing that frees you to move away from the past and move ahead with your life.

For most, the pain will not go as deep as Cindy's tragedy, but the impact of an injury caused by parents can still be felt decades later. The critical question is, how will you respond to your parents' failures and mistakes?

Obviously, many children respond by refusing to forgive their parents. Here are some reasons why.

Excuse #1: "They need to be punished."

We sometimes react to our parents' neglect of us as children by saying, in effect, "When I had needs as a child, you weren't there. Now that you have needs, I'm not going to be there for you." So we punish our parents.

We punish them for withholding acceptance and only giving it when we performed to their standards. We punish them for yelling and screaming at us when we were children. We punish them because when we wanted to talk about problems we were facing at school, they didn't have time to listen. We punish them for laughing at us when they should have understood us. We punish them for not being there—for not playing ball with us, for not taking us fishing, for ignoring us while they watched television. We punish them for dividing our family by divorcing each other.

We punish because we have been hurt deeply. We are angry. And we want our parents to feel some of the white-hot heat.

The desire for revenge, however, traps you in a deadly time loop in which you repeat the events of the past over and over. Consider the story of Sandy, who struggled for years with her mother's selfish and controlling behavior.

During a Thanksgiving visit, Sandy experienced the typical frustrations and pressure. From the moment her family arrived at her parents' home, she devoted all her time to watching her toddler, who loved to pick up small objects. She tried to convince her mother to put anything fragile and expensive out of reach, but her mother said, "This is my home and I'm going to keep it the way I like it. That child should know by now that he shouldn't touch anything."

For the next few hours, that comment simmered in Sandy's mind. *Who does she think she is, telling me I'm not a good mother? Has she forgotten what it's like to take care of a toddler?*

Sandy avoided her mother and hardly spoke to her. Naturally her mother noticed, and naturally that made her angry.

When Sandy finally put her child down for a nap, she decided to lie down herself. That didn't last long, however, because soon she looked up to find her mother glowering in the doorway. "Are you planning to give me any help in the kitchen or do you plan on lying around all day? I can't do it all, you know."

"Mom," Sandy replied, "do you realize that not everybody in this world jumps up to attention when you give orders? I'm tired of you always telling me what to do! I am twenty-eight years old, and I'm doing a good job as a mother. And if you want to see me more often you need to loosen up."

Do you see the cycle? Sandy's mother angered her, so Sandy retaliated by maintaining a wall of silence. This behavior increased the tension, so the mother responded by hurting Sandy again. That, in turn, sparked additional anger in Sandy, which caused her to make a critical comment.

Trying to punish a parent is a no-win option.

Excuse #2: "They need to earn my forgiveness."

There are two problems with this attitude. First, the parent who wounded you may never be able to repay you for the damage caused. Second, why should you give this person control over the situation?

You may suffer for years—emotionally and physically—waiting for repentance that may never come.

Someone has said, "The longer you carry a grudge, the heavier it gets." There are many things that can exhaust a person's resources over a lifetime, but none more draining than anger. I can think of much better ways to expend my life than staying angry at my parents.

Excuse #3: "If I forgive them, they'll feel I'm letting them get away with what they've done."

This excuse often results from the misconception that forgiveness erases the past. It does not.

Forgiveness does not mean excusing or condoning someone's sin. It does not mean smoothing things over.

Forgiveness does not mean forgetting a person's sin. In fact, according to writer Lewis Smedes, "We do the miracle when we remember and then forgive."[2]

Forgiveness does not mean excusing or condoning someone's sin.

Forgiveness does not mean denying you have felt pain, hurt, and anger.

Forgiveness does not mean stuffing your grief. And forgiveness does not mean instant, full reconciliation. Reconciliation is possible with time and effort by both parties to restore trust. However, the process requires maturity and humility that may not be present in your parents. Some parents simply have too much baggage of their own to ever humble themselves to the degree that would allow reconciliation of your relationship.

Forgiveness doesn't erase the past, but it does allow you to break free from the cycle of hurt and anger. It gives you the freedom to begin creating a new future. "Forgiving creates a new possibility of fairness by releasing us from the unfair past," Smedes wrote. "A moment of unfair wrong has been done; it is in the inevitable past. If we choose, we can stick with that past. And we can multiply its wrongness. If we do not forgive, our only recourse is revenge. But revenge glues us to the past. And it dooms us to repeat it."[3]

Excuse #4: "I'm fearful about how they will respond if I tell them I forgive them."

Offering forgiveness to parents means talking about the past. Will the parents respond with anger? Will they deny their sins and mistakes? Will they try to manipulate and twist the forgiveness to their own advantage?

It's true that you can't control how your parents will respond. A friend wrote to tell me that soon after becoming a follower of Christ, he knew God wanted him to forgive his father for abusing him as a child. But when he did, the father responded, "Just forgive yourself."

"I felt so angry and betrayed for an instant," my friend wrote. "I wanted to curse, but in the next instant God reminded me that I had done all He had asked me to do. I was obedient and I was free." During the next few years, God used that act of obedience to build a stronger relationship between father and son.

Fear prevents many people from working through issues with their parents. We feel so fragile that we cannot face the possibility of being hurt again. We fear rejection so much that we would rather live in its grip than go to those who have offended us.

Being controlled by fear is actually a failure to love. First John 4:18 says, "There is no fear in love, but perfect love casts out fear. For fear has to do with punishment, and whoever fears has not been perfected in love." But the pain of avoidance is no substitute for the peace that comes from having done what is right. By breaking the cycle of bitterness and unresolved conflict through forgiveness, you also allow your relationships to start fresh.

Looking at God's Example

In Ephesians 4:31–32, the apostle Paul commanded Christians to "Let all bitterness and wrath and anger and clamor and slander be put away from you, along with all malice." Instead, Paul says, we are to "be kind to one another, tenderhearted, forgiving one another, just as God in Christ forgave you."

This raises two interesting questions: Why did you need forgiveness, and what did God in Christ do to forgive you?

To answer these questions I would like to take you to a pivotal moment in human history: the crucifixion of Jesus Christ as described in Luke 23. It's a story that is rich in significance.

After Christ was betrayed, after He was tried and convicted unfairly, after He was humiliated and scourged and jeered and spat upon, He finally suffered the cruelest indignity. The only perfect man who ever lived was hung on a cross between two criminals. Looking on, soldiers mocked Him and shouted, "If you are the King of the Jews, save yourself!"

Forgiveness initiates.

Yet Christ's response was incredible. Even at that moment, while suffering the most terrible abuse, He said, "Father, forgive them, for they know not what they do."

Learn four crucial lessons from this story.

The first is that forgiveness embraces the offenders. Christ offered forgiveness to the very people who hurt Him the most. And that's not all. He offered it to them while they were still hurting Him. In the same way, your sins are a direct affront, an obscenity, to a holy God, and yet He still forgives you.

The second is that forgiveness initiates. God desired your fellowship so much He took the initiative in forgiving you. He did not wait for you to earn forgiveness. Romans 5:8 reads, "But God shows his love for us in that while we were still sinners, Christ died for us."

The third lesson is that forgiveness gives up all rights to punish.

God canceled your debt against Him. You deserve to die as the penalty for your sins. But God, knowing it was absolutely impossible for you to pay that debt, had Christ pay the penalty as a substitution for you. As Colossians 2:13–14 says,

> And you, who were dead in your trespasses and the uncircumcision of your flesh, God made alive together with him, having forgiven us all our trespasses, by canceling the record of debt that stood against us with its legal demands. This he set aside, nailing it to the cross.

Finally, the fourth lesson is that forgiveness is based on reality. One of the criminals hanging alongside Christ recognized He was the Son of God, and he called out, "Jesus, remember me when you come in your kingdom!" Christ replied, "Truly, I say to you, today you will be with me in Paradise." Jesus forgave this criminal of his debt to God, but there is one thing He did not do. He did not allow the man to escape the earthly penalty for his sins.

May I ask you a question? Do you know the love of God? Have you personally experienced the forgiveness of God for your sins? It's available right now to you personally—God's free gift of forgiveness and the promise of eternal life, *if* you surrender in faith to Him and ask for His forgiveness. Almighty God punished His Son for your sin so that you can be forgiven, become His child, and know your heavenly Father. Why not pause right now and settle this issue with God? You'll never be able to forgive your parents if you have not personally received God's forgiveness of you.

In the same way, forgiving your parents means canceling their debt against you, but it does not mean absolving them of other responsibilities. Your parents may need to work hard to regain your trust. In fact, you may need to confront them at some point with their sin and set some requirements that need to be met in order to restore a relationship with you.

You have chosen to release them of their debt to you personally, but for their own good they will need to make choices of their own in order to rebuild their lives.

Just as understanding is seeing a person through the eyes of Christ, and just as compassion is feeling with the heart of Christ, forgiveness is releasing someone from his debt to you . . . like Christ did.

Steps to Forgiveness

If you still struggle with forgiving a parent, however, I would suggest that you try the following. It is not a magic potion, but it can move you a step closer to the point where you are able to forgive your mom or dad as God has forgiven you.

1. Get alone. Spend a day by yourself with your Bible in prayer. I would suggest setting aside at least four to five hours, because often it takes over an hour just to clear your mind of other distractions so you can truly focus on the process God may have for you.
2. Thank God for your parents. Faith pleases God (Hebrews 11:6). Thanking God for your parents—for who they were and were not, and for what they did right and wrong—demonstrates faith. It does not mean you have to feel thankful, only that you can as an act of faith say to God, "Thank You for my parents."

   A friend of mine shared how giving thanks to God for his parents was so important. He told me, "I thank God for my mom and dad. I can say, 'Thank You, God,' for my alcoholic father, because God says in Romans 8:28, 'And we know that God causes all things to work together for good to those who love God.' "

   He concluded, "I believe I have become a better dad, a better husband, and a better man because of my mom and dad. He will cause all things to work together for good."

3. Write out a list of offenses. Some people have taken a sheet of paper and written out how their parents failed them. I would encourage you to begin this time in prayer, asking God to help you call to mind those things that you specifically need to deal with.
4. In prayer, yield. Give up your rights to punish your parents for their offenses. Write across the front of your list of offenses: "I choose today to relinquish all rights to punish. I give them up. I release them from their debt." Reading Ephesians 4:31–32 will help give you some needed perspective.

   The process does not end there, however. For many, the act of forgiveness may need to continue over a period of time until their feelings begin to change. Read on for further suggestions.
5. Process this with a close friend. After you have spent your day alone, you may find it very helpful to discuss what you have done with a trusted friend or your spouse. Share the process, your feelings, and your conclusions.
6. When the temptation to punish your parents arises in the future, admit those feelings and, again, give up the right to punish them. Forgiving another person is a process that continues each time you are reminded of an offense or hurt again. We have to choose to forgive an infinite number of times.

"Anger Was Eating Away at Me"

Your job is to deal with your response to your parents, not their response to you. Romans 12:18 admonishes us, "If possible, so far as it depends on you, live peaceably with all." You do not have total responsibility for the relationship. You may do everything right and still not experience complete healing in the relationship.

Melissa is one woman who confronted her responsibility to forgive her mother. While she was growing up, her mother ruled the house as a strict disciplinarian. She was an extreme perfectionist; there was one right way to do things, and that was her way.

For example, before Melissa came downstairs for breakfast, her room had to be perfectly clean, even the socks and shirts in her drawers had to be perfectly folded and arranged by color. "I always knew if the president ever gave an award for the cleanest home we would win," Melissa said.

Melissa grew up with a great deal of insecurity because she never felt she could please her mother. "I knew she cared for me, but I thought I was not a good kid because I could never do anything well enough to please her. I wanted her to like me and love me. But I never heard her say she loved me as I grew up."

Your job is to deal with your response to your parents, not their response to you.

As Melissa matured into an adult, it took many years to change the relationship. She recalls when she was about twenty-one, sitting on the patio with her mother, and saying, "Mom, what I really wish is that we could get to the point where we could be friends. I'm just about on my own now. I know I could never have been here without you and Daddy, but I was wondering if someday we could step out of that role as mother-daughter and try to be more friends?"

"We will never be friends," her mother replied. "As long as you live, my job will be to be your mother."

Melissa struggled through the years with anger. Her mother continued to criticize her and offer her opinions on everything from marriage to finances to which clothes she should wear. But her relationship with Christ, Melissa said, has given her greater freedom, because being assured of His love has helped release her from the need to be approved by her mother.

That relationship with God also has given her the ability to forgive. "The key has been understanding how much God has forgiven me for things and feeling that grace in my life. I realized that anger was just eating away at me and the only way I could get rid of that was to give it to God in prayer and give her the grace He had given me."

Melissa was pleased to see her mother begin to change during the last few years. "She tells me that she loves me now, and she never did that before. Lately her actions have shown me that she wants to be more like friends. She'll talk to me more as she would talk to her friends, about things going on in her life. I can tell that our relationship has really evolved."

(11)

SEEKING YOUR PARENTS' FORGIVENESS

Forgiveness is the fragrance the violet sheds on the heel that crushed it.

—MARK TWAIN

When Elizabeth became a Christian, she learned how to love others with the love of God. Except for her father. Whenever she considered God's commandment to honor her parents, she'd think, *Surely God has not met my dad. Surely He would not ask me to do that.*

This went on for several years, until the day she heard a speaker say, "If you have bitterness in your heart toward anyone, you need to ask them to forgive you." Thus began a conversation between Elizabeth and her Lord.

God: "You need to ask your dad to forgive you."

Elizabeth: "In the first place, I don't talk to my dad. In the second place, we don't talk about forgiveness. In the third place, I never see him. And in the fourth place, I don't want to do this!"

God: "You need to ask your dad to forgive you."

Elizabeth: "I'll tell You what, God. I'll ask Daddy to forgive me if You bring him here."

She thought she was safe with that prayer because her dad never came to the city where she lived. But the very next day, her mother called and said, "Elizabeth, your uncle is sick, and we are here in town at the hospital."

Even as she drove to the hospital, Elizabeth kept bargaining with God: "Lord, surely You don't want me to ask Daddy to forgive me. But if You do, God, I pray that he'll be alone.

She walked into the lobby, and there sat her father, by himself. Reluctantly, she dragged herself over to him and said, "Daddy, may I speak to you?"

"Yes, Elizabeth," he replied.

"Daddy, God has convicted me that I've been bitter and sarcastic and that I've not honored you. I wonder if you can find it in your heart to forgive me."

To her complete astonishment, her unemotional father began to cry. "Baby, thanks for saying that. It's broken my heart."

Elizabeth realized God wanted to work through her to make a difference. "He can take things that the world says never can happen, or never would happen, and He can make them happen," she says. "He wants us to believe Him."

That event marked the beginning of a true healing in Elizabeth's relationship with her father.

Oiling the Rusty Hinge

If forgiveness helps free people to experience a deeper relationship, then it's important for us as children to consider that we can hurt our parents just as they hurt us. Therefore, we may need to approach them and ask for their forgiveness. For some people, like Debbie, this act of humility is like oiling a rusty hinge, allowing the door that has separated two people to freely swing open.

Have you ever considered that your parents may have legitimate complaints about how you've treated them? Sometimes these offenses are small, sometimes major, but you can bet they remember them.

I remember my wedding day. I was staying at Barbara's house and her father tried to coax me out of their house that morning because it was bad luck to see the bride. "I don't believe in bad luck," I replied, undoubtedly very piously. "There's no theological basis for that."

Boy, was that a stupid comment! Totally unnecessary. My father-in-law never said anything, but I realized later that I should have deferred to his tradition rather than trying to correct what I deemed a theological inaccuracy.

Children of All Ages Hurt Parents

It's easy to understand how children can be oblivious in parceling out hurt to parents. A child's nature is self-centeredness squared. The intensity of a child's selfishness and how it affects a parent may not always be the same as she grows through different stages, but it hurts just the same.

> *By disregarding our parents' feelings and needs we can continue to dishonor them. And hurt them deeply.*

As a five-year-old I embarrassed my parents by announcing that my mom had tied me up for three months. It had actually been only thirty minutes, and I deserved the penalty. That story became a joke in our home, sort of a classic memory. But things changed when puberty hit. Gone was the little boy with his front teeth missing. In his place was an expressive, impulsive, and emotionally explosive teenager.

My parents' rules made me angry. Like a little prosecutor, I gave them all the reasons why I ought to be able to go and do what "everybody else does." When Dad told me I couldn't drive more than five miles on my first night after earning my driver's license, I unhooked the speedometer cable. I lied to them and got caught. I stole from them (pocket change) and didn't get caught. Just to think of it now, well, it must have hurt them.

That was when I was a child. But as adult children we can continue hurting our parents. By disregarding our parents' feelings and needs we can continue to dishonor them. And hurt them deeply.

Common Ways Adult Children Offend Their Parents

I gathered some comments from adults who described some of the ways they've hurt their parents. Here's what they said:

> I'm adopted, and I remember once in an argument telling my parents that they weren't my parents. It really hurt them and I have regretted it to this day.
>
> I didn't go see my father when he was in the hospital with a broken hip. I was waiting for another month when I would see him on a planned Christmas vacation. He died unexpectedly.
>
> I tried to force my newfound faith in Jesus Christ down my parents' throats. I was very judgmental and full of a preachy attitude.
>
> My mother had planned to stay several weeks with me. I don't like anyone smoking in my house. I told her this. She smokes, so she went home.
>
> I got married in spite of the fact that my father tried to tell me I should reconsider the person.
>
> I forgot my dad's birthday because I was wildly infatuated with a guy at the time. I apologized, but I think it really hurt his feelings because the next year he didn't call me on my birthday.

How to Seek Forgiveness from Your Parents

For many who read these pages, it will not be necessary to go to your parents and ask for forgiveness. For a very small number who come from very abusive, evil situations, going to your parents to seek forgiveness might be dangerous. You'll need to seek counsel before going, and if you go, you may need to take a friend or your spouse with you. And for others, honoring your parents will mean that you need to begin by taking responsibility for your own wrong actions and attitudes. Asking for their forgiveness may be the first step toward healing your relationship.

Here are some suggestions to consider:

First, ask God for direction as you go through this process. The Bible compares us to sheep. We need to be occasionally prodded to keep us going in the right direction. Some sheep want to be told, step-by-step, exactly what to do. But only the Good Shepherd knows the intimate details of you, your parents, and your family. He will guide you as you go through the process. So, as I give you some guidance in handling your situation, let me encourage you to go to the Lord and ask Him for guidance and wisdom.

Ask Him to search your heart and reveal how you have offended your parents. The psalmist prayed, "Search me, O God, and know my heart! Try me and know my thoughts! And see if there be any grievous way in me, and lead me in the way everlasting!" (Psalm 139:23–24).

By the way, if nothing comes to mind, don't feel guilty and try to manufacture some meaningless or insignificant offense.

Second, approach your parents and ask them to forgive you. I would not recommend going through a long list of things you've done wrong, asking specifically for forgiveness for each item. As I've watched adult children ask parents for forgiveness, I've observed that specific confession often isn't necessary. Going back in time and restating and reliving deeply damaging events can sometimes do more harm than good. Instead, go with an attitude of humility and honor that says, "I've been wrong in my attitude toward you. I love you and want to honor you. Will you forgive me for not being the son or daughter I should have been?"

Be sure not to use this occasion to condemn your parents or exhort them to seek *your* forgiveness for anything they've done wrong. If that's necessary, do it another time.

Also, if you're planning to write a tribute for them, make sure you ask their forgiveness beforehand. You could consider doing it through a letter or phone call if appropriate. If not, ask forgiveness face-to-face on a separate day from the one you've planned for the tribute.

> *Go with an attitude of humility and honor that says, "I've been wrong in my attitude toward you. I love you and want to honor you. Will you forgive me for not being the son or daughter I should have been?"*

Third, leave the results to God. This includes your parents' response, or lack of it. The vast majority of parents stand ready to forgive and move on. They do not want to further punish you, but only to love you. First Peter 4:8 describes how parents have had to handle their sons' and daughters' imperfections: "Love covers a multitude of sins."

But that's no guarantee. Seeking forgiveness can be risky. Some parents may not be healthy enough spiritually or emotionally to grant forgiveness. Some may not be willing to forgive. The current of mistrust may run so deep in some families that you may have to prove you are sincere. Still others may not want to forgive because that means they have to deal with their responsibility toward you as well.

As you go to your parents, keep your expectations in check. In listening to a number of stories of adult children going to their parents I'm amazed at how stoic most parents are in these situations. They are too reserved to express how meaningful it is to have a son or daughter seek them out for forgiveness and pursue a relationship. I know of one father who called his daughter two months after their meeting to finally say a simple thank you.

The Blessing of Obedience

A friend of mine, Ney Bailey, once described how she became convicted of her need to honor her dad. As she began to process how she would do this, she realized she needed to ask him to forgive her for how she had treated him.

Ney was emotionally abandoned by her father when she was three years old. Hurt gave way to anger, and anger grew into an intense resentment. As a teenager, Ney sometimes went into her parents' bedroom and opened a drawer that held her dad's shirts and his revolver. "I used to stand there beside the bed he slept in, hold that revolver in my hands, and think about murdering my dad."

As an adult, Ney began to look at her father through God's eyes. She began to learn things about the family he grew up in. She began to understand. Soon she felt herself beginning to accept him rather than judge him. Then she decided to go to her parents' home for vacation. "I remember one day in particular. We were sitting in the living room together. I was on the couch, and Daddy was in his reclining chair in front of the TV. Soon he fell asleep. I looked over at him in his chair for a long time and then said in a soft whisper, 'Daddy, I love you and I accept you just like you are—sitting there in your chair.' "

Their relationship began to change because Ney's attitude toward her dad changed.

Some months later Ney realized she needed to honor her dad by asking his advice on a career decision she was facing and by asking forgiveness for her wrong response to him.

"One Sunday afternoon when I was visiting family, Dad and I were at home alone watching a football game together. I mustered up all the courage I could. Then I asked him for counsel on my career decision. He was extremely helpful, and it went much easier than I expected.

"Then I said, 'Daddy, there's something else I've been thinking about. I harbored a lot of bad attitudes when I was growing up, attitudes of ungratefulness and lack of love. I realize how wrong I was, and I'd like to ask you to forgive me. Will you forgive me?' "

He turned to her with a twinkle in his eye and replied, "No." He said he didn't remember much of what she had done.

So Ney said, "Well, will you forgive me for the things you can remember?"

"Yes," he answered.

Before Ney left home her father expressed interest in her work, schedule, and when she'd be home again. All things he'd never shown the slightest bit of interest in before.

A couple days later Ney talked with her mom on the phone and asked, "Did Daddy say anything to you about our visit?"

"Yes," her mom replied. He had exclaimed, "Ney must be losing her mind! She asked me for some advice."[1]

Ney later shared her love for her parents further by writing a five-page tribute to them on their wedding anniversary. And when he died she was at peace with her father.

When a person dares to obey God, great things can happen. I cannot guarantee your parents will respond like Ney's father if you ask for their forgiveness. But God can take your obedience and use it in ways you never dreamed. He has always been the God of "all things are possible."

(12)

THE POWER OF PUBLIC HONOR

All that I am or hope to be I owe to my angel mother. I remember my mother's prayers and they have always followed me. They have clung to me all my life.

—Abraham Lincoln

Most of us are aware of how technology has affected our lives and our family relationships during the past century. The inventions of radio, movies, and television rapidly changed us to a more verbal, superficial, image- and feeling-oriented society. A flood of communication and information overwhelmed us and trivialized many of the important things in life.

And the rise of digital technology—computers, the Internet, cellphones, large-screen televisions, wireless technology, etc.—has only accelerated this trend. We boast about becoming more connected, and yet there is a growing sense that people are becoming so attached to their digital devices that they are losing their most important connections to the important people in their lives.

In this culture, a written document can carry special power. That's why I'm encouraging you to put together a tribute—a formal, public document honoring your parents.

A Tribute Is Special

I can hear the questions now: Won't a letter be enough? Isn't it enough just to stay in touch and spend time with them?

Those are great ways of honoring your parents, but there is something special about a tribute. A public document makes a statement that a letter does not.

By recalling shared experiences and happy memories, a tribute can peel away the veneer and allow people to be vulnerable and truly connect emotionally.

People love to be praised. A formal document, hung in a place of honor in the home, gives your parents something to show off to their friends. My mom has shown the tribute I wrote for her to the cable television repairman and the plumber. She likes to brag that the telephone repairman asked for a copy.

A woman approached me at a conference and told about the tribute she had written for her parents. "They live in a very, very nice home and everything on their walls is artwork," she said. "The thing that showed me that it was meaningful to them was that they put it up in their house. My husband and I joke that they just put it up when we come over, but we've been over there a couple times when they weren't expecting us, and there it was, up on the wall."

A tribute conveys a message from one heart to another. So many people seem to live their lives on the plain of repetition and superficiality. By recalling shared experiences and happy memories, a tribute can peel away the veneer and allow people to be vulnerable and truly connect emotionally, even for only a few minutes. How many moments like that do we experience with our parents in their lifetime?

If you come from a family who buried emotions, the idea of writing a tribute and reading it to your parents may unnerve you. My response to most would be, "I understand the risk and vulnerability of the presentation, but I'd strongly encourage you to do it anyway." It could be that you need to get beneath the surface, just once, to deepen your relationship.

A Turning Point for Her Family

Janelle grew up in the rural south, in a farming family with four brothers and three sisters. Her father worked a large farm, growing cotton and soybeans and raising cattle. Janelle's mother supervised her daughters in keeping up a garden that provided much of the family's food.

Janelle had a happy family, and she didn't recall many family problems growing up. But the one ingredient that seemed to be missing was the ability to express love and intimate feelings to one another.

When Janelle attended a Weekend to Remember alumni session, she felt her heart stirring when she was challenged to write a tribute to her parents. A few months later, her parents briefly separated. Some of the siblings divided, taking sides with one parent or the other. It caused some unnecessary things to be said. Bad feelings lingered, leaving some of them not speaking to each other.

Three weeks before Christmas, her mother called and said, "You're the only ones who won't be here for Christmas this year." That's when Janelle knew the time had come to write her tribute. She and her husband rearranged their plans.

Janelle now had to write the tribute she had been putting off for months. One night, as she sat down to write Christmas cards, she began recalling many different parts of her childhood. "As I jotted them down, it all began to come together. Just in a short time, there was the tribute I had prayed about," she recalled.

Janelle prayed that God would use the tribute to somehow start a healing process for the entire family. On Christmas Day they gathered together, and after the other gifts were opened Janelle stood to present her tribute. "I had prayed the Lord would allow me to read it aloud, because I knew it wouldn't be the same if I had my husband read it. The Lord granted me the ability to do that. I would read a verse, and then emotions would take over, then I'd regroup and start again."

All the grandkids sat spellbound as Janelle read. When she finished, everyone sat in silence. It seemed like a sacred moment. Even after a brother-in-law broke the silence with a funny remark, the emotion remained.

Janelle's parents expressed their appreciation and love, but she was especially pleased by the way her siblings began to talk again as the day progressed. "I can't say that the tribute was totally responsible, but I think it brought everyone to a point of softness. It was like that day was just a turning point.

"God knew what was going to happen during the year to come. He placed a desire in me ahead of time so I could pray. I praise Him for bringing our family together that day to begin healing."

Marble Tributes

Westminster Abbey in London is a grand structure where thousands of people are memorialized in marble tributes and buried in the floor and walls. When I had the privilege of wandering around in that massive cathedral, it was fascinating to see lives described in two dozen words, words that were often quite profound. Kings were honored for leadership, warriors acclaimed for courage, statesmen and writers for their contribution to England.

As I walked among those marble tributes, I couldn't help but wonder why our burial stones here in the United States rarely say anything about a person's life, what he lived for. Most gravestones in this country simply bear the name of the deceased and the dates of birth and death. I think of what my friend Crawford Loritts says about gravestone inscriptions: "An entire life is summarized by a dash between two dates."

Isn't a life worth more than a dash? Perhaps a portion of your tribute will someday make it onto your parents' gravestone to remind descendants and succeeding generations how to invest their lives. Your tribute may never be etched in marble or granite, but if it is a framed, public document hanging in a home, it will always be a reminder to all who read it.

A Tribute from Barbara Rainey to Her Parents, Bob and Jean Peterson, of Camden, Arkansas

My wife, Barbara, took special care in preparing her tribute to her parents, matting it with lace and ribbons intertwined, and presenting it to them as a Christmas gift. She knew God's desire for her to honor her parents, and she wanted to show them her appreciation in a tangible way.

Barbara has seen that honoring her parents has helped to dismantle miscommunications that had occurred in the past.

On Christmas Day in 1987, after all the regular gifts were unwrapped, I took our kids into another room so Barbara could be alone with her parents. I could barely hear her as she read it, and I could tell she was nervous—I've never heard her read anything so fast!

By the time Barbara was finished, all three were crying. It was a holy and unforgettable moment.

Barbara's parents immediately hung the tribute in their kitchen, where it remains today. Since then, Barbara has seen that honoring her parents has helped to dismantle miscommunications that had occurred in the past. It also has opened up opportunities for Barbara to enjoy her relationship with her parents even more and to see them grow together in a solid friendship.

As a side benefit, my relationship with my in-laws has benefited, too. When Barbara honored them, I think they felt like I was honoring them as well. And I did; I was part of it.

This is what Barbara wrote:

> One of my most vivid and pleasant memories is of us kids watching you both work and working with you. As I look back, much of the work I remember was seasonal. With Mom I remember weeding, working, and planting flower beds in the spring. Dad supervised us when he took down storm windows, and we kids got the screens, lined them up against tree trunks to be washed, rinsed, and hung in anticipation of the warm summer days to come. In the summer there was flower-bed maintenance and lawn work to do. I remember my job was to trim the edges of the driveway and sidewalks with the hand clippers. When fall arrived there were leaves to be raked and storm windows to be returned to their protective duty. And then, as the snows came, our shovels kept the sidewalks and driveway clean.
>
> There were inside duties as well—such as cleaning sinks and learning to wash dishes the right way. Mom taught me to sew, iron, embroider, and to finish what I started. I remember being told more than once, "Anything worth doing is worth doing well." Thank you for the gift of a strong work ethic from both experience and your example.
>
> The gifts of character and common sense are now mine because of your model. I learned to value honesty, respect for my elders, and good manners. You taught me to be conservative

and not wasteful, and to value quality because it would endure.

I'm thankful to you both for the gift of self-confidence. Though my self-esteem faltered during my teen years, you demonstrated that you trusted me, and I always knew you believed in me. I remember your allowing me to do a lot with Jimmy when he was a baby and toddler. I felt at times like he was mine as I fed him, rocked him, talked and played with him, and took him to a carnival with my date when he was only three.

You also expressed trust by allowing me to express my creativity—at your expense! You let me decorate the house at Christmas, arrange flowers in the summer, and fix my room up the way I wanted. But the one that took the cake was when you let me paint the bathroom fire engine red with white-and-black trim—a thing I don't think I'd let my kids do. But I'm very grateful for that expression of trust, because it gave me a greater sense of self-confidence.

Another priceless gift was the gift of a good spiritual foundation. As we faithfully attended church and Sunday school as a family, and as I was encouraged to attend Vacation Bible School in the summers and youth group in the teen years, I learned the central importance of God in my life. Because we were always there, I memorized many of the great Christian hymns, which I love to this day.

Because you loved me, you corrected my grammar, picked up my Kleenexes, and you let me go: to France, to college, and to Dennis. Though many of the details are long since forgotten, I'll always remember how proud I felt as I walked down the aisle with Dad, and you both gave me away in marriage.

The last gift I mention is in no way the least. In fact, it is probably the greatest because it is foundational to all the others: it is the example of your marriage. I cannot recall a single argument or disagreement between you. It was apparent that you loved each other, cared for each other, and liked each other. I never felt insecure or fearful that you would leave one another or get a divorce. I treasure that gift of your good, solid, happy marriage. I attribute a great deal of the success of my marriage to the example I saw in yours.

And so, in this season or giving, some thirty-eight years after you gave me the gift of life, I give you this tribute. With a heart of gratitude, I give you my appreciation, my admiration, and my love.

Your daughter, Barbara
Christmas 1987

(13)

WRITING A TRIBUTE

God gave us memories so we could have roses in December.

—UNKNOWN

Perhaps you are intrigued with this idea of writing a tribute to your parents. Possibly you feel a growing conviction you need to do this. Some of you may have no problem putting words on paper. My guess, however, is you may be asking yourself questions like these:

- How can I write something like this when I don't know what to say?
- How can I write a tribute if I can't remember much about my childhood?
- How can I do this if I'm not a good writer?

I've learned that parents do not care about your gift as a writer or a grammarian. They feel honored by the fact that you are speaking from the heart. To be effective, a tribute must include emotion and a piece of your heart. You can accomplish this as you include special memories—those times of happiness, joy, celebration, and even pain and sadness that recapture how you felt as a child.

When I counsel people on how to create tributes like these, I usually suggest a few simple steps. This approach seems to work well in unlocking a flood of memories and even a surprising burst of creativity.

Step One: Prepare Your Heart

Once you decide to write a tribute for your parents, you should spend some time examining your heart. Take an afternoon to be alone with God. Talk with Him, read His Word, and allow Him to search your heart. As Psalm 139:23–24 says, "Search me, O God, and know my heart! Try me and know my thoughts! And see if there be any grevious way in me, and lead me in the way everlasting!" Here are a few questions to help you:

- Are you willing to look at your parents through the eyes of Christ?
- Are you looking to God, rather than your parents, for approval?
- Are your motives pure? Is giving them honor your goal rather than seeking to manipulate your parents through this gesture in some way?
- Are you prepared to honor them regardless of their response?
- Are you willing to thank God for your parents—for what they've done right and for the influence they've had in your life?
- Are you willing to ask for their forgiveness if needed?
- Are you willing to forgive them for how they have hurt you?

If you responded yes to all these questions, then I encourage you to move ahead with your tribute. It'll be liberating as you begin the process.

In an interview on our daily radio program *FamilyLife Today,* Josh McDowell spoke frankly about learning to thank God for his parents. He said he grew up envying other people's parents. His father was known as the town drunk, and as a teenager Josh was ashamed of him.

Late one night, when Josh was in his early thirties, more than a dozen years after he had become a Christian, he thanked God for his mom and his dad and forgave them—even though they were no longer living. Josh said, "It was the first time I thanked God for my parents. . . . It was as if God said, 'Josh, who do you think I have used most in your life, whether good or bad, to make you who you are?' I had to admit it was my mother and father.

"God says in Romans 8:28 He will cause all things to work together for good to those who love Him and are called according to His name," Josh concluded. "I believe I had become a better dad and husband because of my mom and dad. He will cause—and has caused—all things to work together for good."

Step Two: Create a Memory List

Your goal here is to collect as many memories as you can. Write down the good memories you have about your childhood—events, happy occasions, interesting experiences with your family, things your parents taught you, and more. Don't try to edit what you write down or to be selective at this point; you want to pull memories out of your mind and put them on paper. This is like priming a pump; you just need to get a little flow started.

You might want to start with an hour alone, just writing down anything you can remember. Then, over the next few weeks, carry around a notepad or some index cards to write down anything that comes to mind, or record voice memos in your phone. You will be surprised how, once you start, little things will spark memories—smells, sights, things people say, things your kids do, and so on.

Here's what I can promise you: God will help you remember some good memories. Don't be afraid if the memories don't come right away. Some have shared with me that they took the better part of a year to collect these experiences.

By telling stories to your wife or your children, you may recover additional details. Or they may ask questions that spark further memories.

If you have trouble remembering what happened in your childhood, or what you can thank your parents for, you may need a little more help priming the pump. Check out the list of "Questions to Help You Unlock Your Memories" in the appendix.

Often a simple question can revive a long-buried memory. My cohost on *FamilyLife Today*, Bob Lepine, helped me brainstorm the list in the appendix, and the question, "What activities did they participate in with you?" led him to say: "This reminds me of when I was in eighth or ninth grade and I spent a week at Boy Scout Camp with my dad. He was there as the Scoutmaster more than he was there as my dad, and I don't remember that we got any emotional closeness or bonding or anything out of that. But I was just realizing he took a week of vacation to do that. That's a sacrifice."

As you are recalling memories, it also helps to talk with other people. By telling stories to your wife or your children, you may recover additional details. Or they may ask questions that spark further memories.

For the person who is still stumped and seems to be finding the memory well empty, a phone call to a brother, sister, aunt, or uncle may help get things going.

Step Three: Write the Tribute

Before you begin, pray. Ask God to help you; empower you; and fuel your mind, your words, and the entire process. If He can raise His

Son from the grave (and He did!), He can help you find the words that will enable you to truly honor your parents.

If you are writing to two parents, one basic decision you will need to make is whether you want to write two individual tributes or one tribute to both. There's no right or wrong here; it all depends on the occasion and what you feel comfortable doing.

There are many formats you can use to present your material, including a scrapbook, a book, a notebook, or a framed picture. The format you choose will help determine the length and look of your written material. For the rest of this chapter, however, I am going to concentrate on the format I think works especially well: a typeset and framed document.

After you have finished your memory list, you may end up with dozens of items. You will need to reduce the length to fit whatever word length you have chosen for your framed picture, so now it is time to prioritize.

Go through the list and select the memories you feel are most important to include in the tribute. Choose the memories that are the most meaningful and emotionally vivid to you. Also, be sure to include items that your parents would appreciate most.

When you start writing, don't worry about being fancy. Just tell the story as if you are talking to a friend.

You might want to start off with a statement telling why you have written this tribute. For example, "Too often we let our lives go by and we fail to let the ones who are most important to us know just how special they are. You are special. There are so many reasons I am thankful that you are my daddy."

Then try to turn each memory you have selected into a sentence or paragraph. For example, memories like "Good provider, hard worker, went to work even when he was sick or when it was icy outside, paid my way through college, always got me cars" could be turned into a paragraph like this:

> I never, ever worried that I wouldn't have the things I needed or wanted, because you are such a hard worker. I can remember days you went to work even when you didn't feel good and a few times you had to walk to work because of icy roads. And, unlike many parents, you paid my way through college. Even provided a car. I can never remember hearing you complain about the drain it probably put on your pocketbook.

At the end, conclude with a special note of thanksgiving and appreciation, such as

> Thank, You, Lord, for giving Thomas M. (Jim) Dodd as a daddy to me and a papa to my children. You knew what You were doing when You gave him to us.

After you have written this first draft, read through it another time, looking for ways to improve it. Does everything make sense? Is the writing clear enough to understand what you are describing?

It also helps to have another person—a friend or your spouse—look at your tribute, because he or she may spot some problems you haven't thought of. If you are concerned about grammar and spelling, it might be a good idea to ask a friend to look it over for you.

Step Four: Print and Frame the Tribute

You'll need to create a clean version of the document, suitable for framing. Here are a few suggestions:

- Use a word processing or publishing app to set your document in the font you desire. Print it on a laser printer. Be sure to use a font large enough so your parents (and their friends) can read it easily. You may need to adjust the length of your document so it will fit in the frame you've chosen.

- You may wish to formalize your document and have it professionally laid out by an artist or designer.
- Hire a calligrapher to craft the document and give it a classy look, but make sure the art doesn't get in the way of the words, making it difficult to read.
- Decide if you want to add any photos, artwork, or other mementos to the document and plan accordingly.

When you choose your frame and matting, consider using UV-filtering glass. This will help prevent fading. A store-bought frame usually doesn't include this type of glass, but it can be replaced by a frame shop at a reasonable cost. When your parents are gone, you will want this document as a keepsake to hang in your home. Both of my parents are now gone and I have both of my tributes hanging in my office.

Step Five: Present the Tribute to Your Parents

Rather than just giving your parents your tribute, present it to them. I'm going to say this one more time for emphasis: Don't ship your tribute to your parents—take it to them and read it.

Consider presenting it publicly. I suggest doing it at a special occasion: a family reunion; anniversary party; a time when the family gathers together around a holiday such as Thanksgiving, Christmas, a birthday, Mother's Day, or Father's Day.

> *Don't ship your tribute to your parents—take it to them and read it.*

Or present it privately. Perhaps you will want to steal away with your mom or dad for a private reading of your tribute. Possibly a trip home for no other reason would etch the message on their hearts permanently. You may have to pull them aside at a family gathering, like Christmas, and read it to them.

Present it with your children watching and listening. Some of the most profound scenes painted in my mind are of a son or a daughter and his or her children all gathered at the feet of parents as the tribute is being read. What better picture can we give the next generation of the profound power of obeying God and His commandments?

A Memorable Experience

Dave Boehi, who assisted me in innumerable ways in the crafting of this book, went home and, along with his sister, Denise, honored his parents on their fortieth wedding anniversary. They prepared a special meal, gave them cards and gifts, and then led them into the living room. They brought their kids in to listen as Denise and Dave read their tributes.

I called him soon after he arrived back home. Dave is a reserved man, and he was surprised at how he reacted as he read the tribute: "I tried to express things in the tribute that I'd never said before, and I got more and more emotional as I read it. I don't think anyone expected me to cry the way I did. My wife and my daughters didn't know what to do—they'd never seen me cry like that. My youngest daughter sat on my lap and kept looking back up at me with surprise on her face. Then she hugged me, wanting me to know everything was okay."

Dave could tell how deeply his parents were touched, but they didn't say anything about the tributes during the following day. But then his mom told him in a private moment that the evening had been the "most memorable experience of my life."

Frogs on a Log

Just do it!

One of my favorite parables I love to tell at our Weekend to Remember marriage getaways has to do with frogs and a log:

If you had five frogs on a log and three of them decided to jump, how many frogs would you have left on the log?

The answer is *five.*

Why? Because there is a difference between deciding to jump and jumping.

Will you write a tribute?
Just do it.

(14)

NO REGRETS

Even now, twenty-one years after my father died, not a week goes by that I don't find myself thinking I should call him.

—Herb Gardner

Ecclesiastes 7:2 tells us, "It is better to go to the house of mourning than to go to the house of feasting, for this is the end of all mankind, and the living will lay it to heart."

These words are a powerful reminder that we need to do the important things while we still have time. It's good to remember that everyone will die. There's nothing like visiting a house of mourning to jerk us to a halt and consider how we've spent our lives.

I once read a quote from former U.S. Senator Paul Tsongas that jolted me into reality. After recovering from his third bout with cancer, Tsongas said:

> It's the dread of being removed from the scene that makes you appreciate being on the scene. If you presume endless days, then no day has particular value.

> I think of all the fathers who have young children and play golf all day Saturday and Sunday. They've never had cancer. I think of the husbands who never voice their affection for their wives. They've never had cancer.[1]

As I consider those words I think about adult children who have never expressed their thankfulness to their parents. They know their parents will die someday. They know they need to make an effort to honor them. But they procrastinate, thinking they can do it later.

No Words Left Unsaid

During the early 1980s, when I first began to speak on honoring parents, I received a letter from a student that put the issue in perspective:

> Dear Dennis:
>
> Your lecture today brought to mind the importance of phone calls to parents. My mother died about one year prior to my enlistment in the Air Force. As I departed New York City bound for San Antonio, Texas, my father took a day off work to see me off on my new adventure. To my knowledge, it was the only day off work he ever took, other than at my mother's funeral, and the only time I saw him cry.
>
> I left with a promise that I would call him every Sunday at 2 p.m. and was faithful to that promise. One Sunday the phone rang for a long time and when Dad finally answered, I was truly concerned that something had gone wrong. Dad assured me all was well.
>
> He seemed to have a lot to talk about that day. He expressed his sorrow at not having been able to spend more time with me as I grew up. I assured him that I understood and all the times we did have together were memorable and meaningful. His closing words were, "I love you and I miss you."

> Those were the last words he spoke to me. Two days later I received a phone call and the voice on the other end said, "Pops is dead." It was later determined that Dad suffered two heart attacks, one conceivably on the day that I had called.
>
> I pray that you will continue to stress contact with parents. However that contact is made, it could be the last opportunity to share your heart with someone who loved you and for you to express that the love was mutual.
>
> [signed] A student thankful for being reminded of a two-way blessing

I like that phrase, "a two-way blessing." That's what honoring your parents is—a blessing to the parent in finally receiving thanks for what he did right and a blessing to the child who can grow old knowing no words were left unsaid.

I know how it feels to have a parent die with words unsaid. My dad died of a heart attack a few days short of his sixty-sixth birthday. I never had the chance to say good-bye. Yes, for a decade prior to his death I had sought to honor him, but I'll always regret that I never expressed it in the same way I did to Mom, with a tribute.

They'll Always Be There, Won't They?

I'd like to challenge you to consider two questions. The first is, Would you have any regrets if your parents died tomorrow?

I know how it is for many adults, especially those in your twenties, thirties, and forties. You feel so consumed by your responsibilities at work, in your marriage, with your children, and at your church. Somehow, in the midst of a busy and hectic schedule, it's easy to leave parents in the dust. *They'll always be there, won't they?* you think. *Once I get past that next deadline . . . once we finish this vacation . . . once the kids grow a little older . . . then I'll spend some time with my parents.*

If your relationship with your parents is difficult—if anything with your parents remains unresolved—it is even easier to shove the problem off to a corner of your mind. Or to convince yourself that you've done all you can do. A friend of mine told me he had a good relationship with his father, but was concerned his sister did not. He asked her, "Would you have any regrets if Dad dies tomorrow? Are you content with it ending this way? And if not, why not do something about it?"

As wonderful as a funeral eulogy can be, I wish I could start a new tradition of praising parents before they die rather than afterward.

Her response? She said she had done all she could do to reconcile with her father. But I wondered if the real problem was that she didn't want to go through the pain and hard work of reconciliation. When her father died, would she find herself struggling with guilt that she didn't make more of an effort?

I know of another man who was motivated to honor a father he had seen only twice since he was ten. "I didn't want to live with the regret that the last time I'd see him was standing over his casket at his funeral. I knew Christ, and he didn't. My responsibility to love him began to grow within me. I might be the only one in my family to share God's love and forgiveness in Christ."

That man has sought to honor his father through numerous visits. And he calls and writes him regularly. Today that man has no regrets.

The second question is, Why wait for the eulogy to praise your parents?

As wonderful as a funeral eulogy can be, I wish I could start a new tradition of praising parents before they die rather than afterward. We need to say it when our words will become nourishment for an old soul, when it will most encourage them. I often wonder how many eulogies are delivered with the hope that parents can *somehow* hear the words.

Dan told my sixth-grade Sunday school class a wonderful story about a lesson his father taught him:

> I recall how, as a child, after church or Sunday school, my father would take me to the cemetery. He would take my hand and we'd walk around and I would ask him, "Daddy, what are you doing?"
>
> He'd say, "Well, I want to go see where my mother and my father were buried."
>
> He would stand there and cry, and I turned to him one day and I said, "Daddy, when I get big, I'll come out and see you in the cemetery."
>
> He turned to me and he said something really outstanding, and it stuck with me all these years. He said, "I don't want you to do that."
>
> I said, "Why?" And he said, "Well, I would rather you give flowers to the living, because when I am dead and gone and I'm out there in the cemetery, I won't be able to smell the flowers you bring me. So I would rather you do nice things to please me while I'm alive."
>
> If nothing else, my father left me a legacy of seeking to honor parents while they are alive. Instead of going through life thinking about what we can get from our parents, what our parents can do for us, and how our parents can help us, we have to—before they die—say, "What can I do for you?" How can I please my parents who have nurtured, raised, cared for, disciplined, and loved me?
>
> If our parents are still alive, no matter what bridges have been burned or doors have been closed, it is our responsibility as children to make the step forward. We must make the move because our parents are sometimes set in their ways. We

are the ones who must come forward and bring a bouquet of flowers while they are still living. We owe it to them and we owe it to God.

If a Parent Already Has Died

This chapter will unearth some difficult emotions for those of you who feel regret over not honoring parents before they died. As I know myself, you may never be able to erase those feelings, but I can offer three suggestions:

First, allow yourself to grieve over the loss of your parent and over your failure to honor. I can still remember sitting at my dad's funeral, with deep grief, but immense pride in a man who was really the bedrock of my early years.

It wasn't until after Dad was gone that I really began to measure the man. Twenty years later I continue to take measurements, and the magnitude of what he left me looms larger in my mind.

Second, make a special effort to honor the living parent as a way of honoring the one who is deceased. By praising the man my mother chose to spend her life with, I was telling her, "Not only was your husband worthy of honor, but you are worthy as well because you made such a wise choice."

Finally, look for ways to honor your deceased parent. Consider that your children will benefit from knowing the legacy their grandfather or grandmother left them. A tribute can be a milestone for them as they begin their pilgrimage through life.

I wrote a tribute to my father nearly ten years after he died, which I feel not only honored him, but also brought healing to me. I have no idea whether those in heaven are able to see what happens here on earth, but I do know he would have been pleased. And I am certain of this: God sees and He is pleased with the tribute I wrote because it honors my dad. The only thing better would have been to give it to him in person.

This is what I wrote:

A TRIBUTE TO "HOOK" RAINEY

"Dad's home," I used to yell as the back door slammed shut.

Our small, two-story frame house would shudder when the back door slammed shut. The sound of the slamming door was especially loud when one man came through its threshold—my dad. I can recall, as a little boy, playing in my room and hearing that door send a series of quakes that rippled through the walls and rattled the windows. It was my dad's signature and signal that a day of work was completed and a man was now home.

I would yell, "Dad's home!" and then dash through the hall and kitchen to greet him with a well-deserved hug. I would then follow him like a little puppy to the wash room where he washed his callused, grimy hands like a "real man." Everything about him signaled he was a "real man"—from the gritty Lava soap to the Vitalis hair tonic and Old Spice aftershave.

My dad was a unique blend of no-nonsense and discipline with a subtle sense of humor. He was a quiet and private man. He was a man of few words, who didn't seem to need many words to get the job done. His countenance commanded respect.

In fact, there were several boys who had a personality and discipline transformation when they graduated from the third grade Sunday school class to my dad's fourth grade class. Miraculously, discipline problems dried up along with dozens of paper spit wads. In the twelve months that followed, paper airplanes were grounded and eight boys sat up straight in their chairs dutifully listening to the lesson.

"Hook" Rainey they used to call him. The tall lefty got his nickname from his curve ball—a pitch so crooked it mystified batters. I got the feeling he was on his way to becoming a legend in his day, he even pitched a game against Dizzy Dean. Funny thing, but he never could remember the score of that memorable game! I used to accuse him of convenient amnesia!

I recall the easy chair that used to carry the shape of his exhausted form. It was as he was reading the evening paper that I usually planned my assault on him. I'm certain I nearly pestered him to death on more than one occasion while asking my weary dad to play catch.

And play catch he did. Night after night, Hook taught me how to throw a curve, slider, and knuckle-ball. He used to claim you could count the stitches on his knuckle-ball, and when he threw that patented knuckler the entire front yard was filled with laughter—his and mine. I always loved to hear him laugh. Somehow it told me everything was secure.

When I was three or so, he went to Colorado hunting and bagged a fierce teddy bear. He staged the action on film and brought the fierce beast back to me. My kids now play with that worn-out, thirty-five-year-old black and white bear.

I watched him look after the needs of his mother—he used to visit his mom three or four times a week. He modeled what it means to honor one's parents.

From him I learned about integrity, trust, and how to be a man of my word. His example taught me the importance of perseverance, for he stuck with his job for nearly forty-five years. He leaves me an indelible imprint of sinking roots down deep, and living with the same people with whom he did business.

When I was in high school, I won the magazine sales contest because I introduced myself as Hook Rainey's son. That was good enough for an instant sale for nearly 100 percent of my customers. My dad had helped so many people that being his son gave me immeasurable credibility. (For a while I actually thought I was a great salesman!)

His reputation was untarnished in the community. His funeral was attended by nearly a third of the small, southwest Missouri community. He lived and did his work all within five miles of where he was born. One man was even able to say about my father, "In all my years I never heard a negative word about Hook Rainey."

He gave me imperishable memories instead of just things: Memories of Little League baseball (he was the coach); fishing trips where he netted my fish, so small they went through the holes in the net; and a clipped collection of all the baseball and basketball scores from my games, of which he never missed one. There are memories of watching him through the frosted window of our old pick-up truck delivering hams at Christmas. Memories of the feel of his whiskers when he wrestled with me on the floor of the living room, and memories of him whispering to me—an extroverted, impetuous boy—not to bother people while they work. And finally, memories of snuggling close to him as we watched the game of the week with Dizzy Dean as the announcer.

As an impressionable young boy, my radar caught more of his life than he ever knew. He was the model and hero I needed during some perilous teenage years. And you know what? He still is. He taught me the importance of hard work and completing a task. I learned about lasting commitment from him; I never feared my parents would divorce. My dad was absolutely committed to my mom. I felt secure and protected.

But most importantly he taught me about character. He did what was right, even when no one was looking. I never heard him talk about cheating on taxes; he paid them and didn't grumble. His integrity was impeccable. I never heard him lie, and his eyes always demanded the same truth in return. The mental snapshot of his character still fuels and energizes my life today.

"Dad's home!" I can still hear the door slam and the house quake.

This morning as I write this, Dad truly is "home"—in heaven. I look forward to seeing him again someday and saying thanks for the legacy he gave me. And mostly for being "my dad."

But right now, you'll have to pardon me. I miss him.

(15)

WHEN THE DAMAGE GOES DEEP

My father was frightened of his father, I was frightened of my father, and I am damned well going to see to it that my children are frightened of me.

—King George V

If your parents were abusive, or if a parent abandoned you, nothing I could say would adequately capture what you've felt as you've made your way this far in the book. The idea of honoring your parents and making the relationship a two-way street seems nearly impossible. Maybe your heartache is so intense you feel I've been insensitive to your situation. Or perhaps you consider the message of this book cruel punishment.

I want to assure you that my encouraging you to honor your parents comes after numerous encounters with victims of abuse. I've counseled, cried, and agonized with both youngsters and adults who feel emotional pain because of the unimaginable.

I remember a teenage girl who slept with her legs crossed because her dad assaulted her almost every night for six years. I've heard stories of a dad who regularly whacked his sons on the face and hands with a two-by-four he kept by the dinner table. I've been to sexual abuse seminars. I've interacted professionally with numerous counselors. The damage goes deep—much deeper than I could ever fathom.

I cannot promise you a happy ending. I can promise you that God knows, understands where you are, and cares.

I realize not everyone comes from a home like the one I grew up in. Some parents were just bad parents. Others were mean, even evil. Wickedness personified.

I realize, too, that not everyone who reads these pages is ready to face his or her abuser, let alone entertain thoughts of somehow honoring such a parent. And I realize some parents might mock any effort to honor them. I cannot promise you a happy ending. I can promise you that God knows, understands where you are, and cares.

Yet for the adult child who was abandoned or abused by his or her parents, the process of honoring those parents—perhaps just by taking the initiative to reestablish a relationship—may be a critical step of profound healing and perhaps even reconciliation.

Trusting in a Sovereign God

Why is moving toward honoring a parent an important process for a child who was abused or abandoned? I can think of several reasons.

1. We need to be obedient to God regardless of our pain.

Humanly speaking, it doesn't seem fair or even logical that God would command victims of emotional, physical, or sexual abuse to honor the parents who abused them. This is hard to understand and often painful to accept. But because the Bible is God's truth and shows us how to live, we are wise to obey Him and follow His direction.

Many abuse victims are led to believe—often by the very people who harm them—that they deserve the abuse and are somehow at fault. Nothing could be farther from the truth. But the victim *is* responsible for something else: how he or she lives the rest of life. Bitterness and rage are certainly understandable in an abuse victim, but ultimately that victim must make a decision whether to allow God to bring comfort and healing. One victim said it this way: "I refuse to allow my abuse and my abuser to define the rest of my life!"

Fortunately, the God of truth is also the God of grace (John 1:14-17). He is the giver of mercy and is patient with us as we process hurts and wounds that no human deserves.

In fact, God has built a track record of taking things that were meant for evil and turning them into something that He uses for good. The Book of Genesis, for example, describes how Joseph's brothers sold him into slavery. But Joseph believed God wanted to use his circumstances for His purposes. Through faith, Joseph saw God's fingerprints all over his life. Later, after God used him to save His people by bringing them to Egypt, Joseph told his brothers, "As for you, you meant evil against me, but God meant it for good, to bring it about that many people should be kept alive, as they are today" (Genesis 50:20).

In the same way God can use your circumstances in an evil world to bring His good to your life. God doesn't cause evil, but He does allow it. And somehow He mysteriously weaves His purposes into our lives through people who are fallen, depraved creatures.

2. We may experience healing by going through the process of honoring our parents.

As we've seen, the process of honoring our parents can help move us from rage and anger, denial and ambivalence to an honest assessment of their fault and our responsibility. Ultimately the pain can move us to a trust in the sovereign God, and we always benefit from trusting God more.

As a teenager and young adult, Christy saw her mother only twice, for a total of fifteen minutes. Her mom couldn't handle the resulting guilt from walking out of her marriage, leaving her husband alone to care for Christy and her two brothers. So she dropped out of their lives.

Her mom missed report cards, scraped knees, cheerleading, graduation, a college scholarship, a life-threatening auto accident, marriage, and the birth of a baby. Her mom's only response to cards, letters, and phone calls was a heart-piercing silence.

Yet Christy had a compelling desire to honor her mother by pursuing a relationship with her. The command of Exodus 20:12 moved Christy over a two-year period to summon up all the courage and faith she could. Finally, she decided to spend a few days with her mom and honor her in some small way.

Christy's brothers quietly questioned the idea. They thought their mother didn't deserve this kind of attention. They thought Christy was a glutton for punishment. But Christy called her mother anyway. And her mom consented to see her.

Christy's feet felt leaden as she walked to the door of her mom's house. No walk from a car to a house ever seemed longer. Her mind was awash with questions, worries, and the risk of further rejection that this face-to-face meeting represented.

"I knew I could get blown out of the water," Christy recalled. "Emotionally I was a wide-open target. My expectations were zero. I did not want to dredge up the past—I had forgiven her for all that. I wanted the opportunity to let her know I loved her and that I regretted not knowing her."

The next few hours with this stranger called "Mom" challenged Christy to the core. Several times she nearly decided to leave because she was bored stiff and had nothing in common with this woman.

Finally, as she prepared to leave, Christy's eyes met her mother's. "Mom, I want you to know that even though I don't agree with what you did, I still love you," she said. "You're still my mother, and no matter what has happened I think it would be good for us to get to know each other better. Would you like that?"

Her mom began to cry and said, "I thought you hated me all these years after what I did to you. I've missed you so much."

A lot of healing took place at that moment, Christy said. "I felt like a ten-year-old girl with her mom. I just wanted to know if she loved me. And she did."

A decade later, Christy had seen the relationship blossom with her mom. She admitted that she had to initiate 90 percent of the calls. Each call was a white-knuckle time of anxiety and knots in the stomach because of the fear of rejection. Yet, each one was emotionally satisfying.

Her mom slowly learned to love and began showing a growing interest in Christy's faith in a God whom she had always disliked.

"It feels good to have swept that area of my life out," Christy said. "I feel whole. I've dealt with a tragedy in my life. I'm no longer controlled by my anger toward my mom."

Christy said she ranked four events in her life as the most life changing: coming to know Christ, marrying her husband, and honoring each of her parents. "Honoring my parents has freed me to love, to forgive, to be forgiven, to love my husband, and to be a mom to my kids." Uncommon obedience can yield unimaginable benefits.

3. Establishing a relationship with a parent may help reconcile that parent to God.

Perhaps the idea of honoring your parents is almost laughable. You may have a parent who seems to have no redeeming value. Perhaps you need to confront this parent about past abuse or abandonment.

Many books written by counselors detail the steps an abuse victim needs to take in order to confront the abuser. But few, even in the Christian community, seem to acknowledge the responsibility to "honor" such parents.

I have no problem with the concept of confronting parents when such confrontation is necessary. But it should be done with the right attitude. I believe honoring parents demands that as you confront them you do it with the desire to help them know Christ as Savior. Rather than demand revenge, a child has to offer love and support—the hope of a relationship. As Dan Allender writes in his book *The Wounded Heart,* "The objective must be to bless the other person rather than to make sure we are not abused again."[1]

Dr. Allender goes on to tell the story of a young man who confronted his father about past sexual abuse. But he also made it clear that he was willing to begin their relationship again if the father repented. The father denied his sin, and eventually the son chose to stop seeing him. The son honored his father by forgiving him and offering a relationship, but he wouldn't allow his dad to continue sinning by denying the abuse.

This is what Allender calls "bold love"—making the effort to restore a person to full life. "He honored his father," Allender writes, "by giving him the opportunity to repent and taste the restoration of relationship with the righteous Father. The door to relationship was closed, but not locked."[2]

Suggestions for Honoring an Abusive Parent

If you are seriously thinking of taking steps to honor an abusive parent, you will need to commit to wrestling honestly with your past—the good and the bad, the joyful and the painful. Denial of reality is a very real enemy. You must wrestle and ultimately deal with the feelings of mistrust, betrayal, and anger.

Following are some suggestions to consider as you begin. I encourage you to talk to your pastor or a mature Christian counselor who can guide you through the process of healing and help protect you from further abuse.

First, acknowledge any emotional shock, fear, and anger you may have at the thought of having to honor your parents. You may be adamantly against this outrageous concept, thinking, *He's crazy if he thinks I'm going to risk more rejection to try to honor them!* Or you may think, *I've already been damaged enough. The safest way to live out my life is to keep my distance from my parents and to protect my heart.*

These are real feelings. Fair feelings. But God calls us to live by faith, not by feelings. He also calls us out of our self-protection and preservation and into self-denial and self-sacrifice in relationships.

Real meaning in life is found in a real relationship with God and with real people. It does not mean living with a layer of insulation around your heart to protect you from further abuse. True relationships demand risk and authenticity. I'm not speaking of going back and placing your life under your parents' control. I'm talking about developing an attitude so that you're able to approach them with an open heart, receptive to both love and pain. Real relationships have both.

The second step is to take an honest inventory of the extent of your abuse. It's interesting how often we want to avoid reality. Some abuse victims pretend their families are perfect and are unwilling to admit or confront past abuse. Others focus solely on the negative and refuse to acknowledge that their parents may have done even a few things well.

Dan Allender summarizes eight truths that a sexual abuse victim must process and admit. Most apply to those who have suffered other forms of abuse as well:

1. I have been abused.
2. I am a victim of a crime against my body and soul.
3. As a victim, I am not in any way responsible for the crime, no matter what I might have experienced or gained as a result of

the abuse.*

4. Abuse has damaged my soul.
5. The damage is due to the interweaving dynamics of powerlessness, betrayal, and ambivalence.
6. My damage is different from others' in extent, intensity, and consequences, but it is worthy to be addressed and worked through no matter what occurred.
7. It will take time to deal with the internal wounds; the process must not be hurried.
8. I must not keep a veil of secrecy and shame over my past. But I am not required to share my past with anyone I feel is untrustworthy or insensitive.[3]

The third step is to thank God by faith for who your parents were and who they weren't in your life. First Thessalonians 5:18 instructs us to give thanks in all things. By doing this in faith, we acknowledge that God never stopped loving us, that He is intimately aware of who we had as parents, and that He knows what He is doing.

Brian's dad had done an average job of providing but a poor job of loving. After Brian became a Christian, he began to realize he needed to give up the anger he felt toward his father. Over a period of months he moved from the murky, toxic waters of bitterness and anger to a clear, honest assessment of what his dad had done right and wrong. Finally, Brian was able to forgive his dad and let go of his bitterness.

Over the next few years, their relationship improved. When his father died, Brian stood by the casket and prayed with a genuine

---

* While this point is true for sexual abuse victims, I believe it may not be completely true for some other forms of abuse. For example, if a teenager provokes a parent to anger, and that parent beats the child, both individuals have made mistakes. The parent should be held accountable for the physical abuse, but the child should not have goaded the parent. I'm not saying the beating was the child's fault—just that he needs to acknowledge his own responsibility in how he treats his parents.

heart, "Thank You, God, for who Dad was and for who he wasn't."

The fourth step is to choose, as an act of your will, to forgive your parents for all the damage they've done to you.

> *Keep on laying aside the desire to be the avenger of your wounds. Let God handle it.*

I still wonder how the command to honor parents is worked out in many difficult, dark situations. When I hear some people talk about what they experienced in the past, I wonder if I would be able to forgive "seventy times seven," as Jesus commanded us.

Keep on laying aside the desire to be the avenger of your wounds. Let God handle it. In Romans 12:19 Paul warned and promised, "Beloved, never avenge yourselves, but leave it to the wrath of God, for it is written, 'Vengeance is mine, I will repay, says the Lord.' "

God is bigger than your parents. You may never see how He handles it, but He is just and He will settle all accounts. It's His promise.

Finally, when you are ready, begin taking steps to honor your parents. For victims of abuse, the process of honoring parents won't be easy. It will involve prayer, immersion in the promises of the Scripture, counsel, and sacrificial obedience—all occurring over a long period of time.

Realize that your parents may refuse to admit their failures and be reconnected. For some adult children, the process of offering forgiveness to their parents and reestablishing a relationship can result in a breakthrough and a real connection with parents. But some parents don't want to take responsibility for their failures. At this point in their lives they may not be able to assume that responsibility. And at your offer of grace and forgiveness, they may become (or remain) mean, evil, hardened people, resisting your love.

Also understand that God commands us to honor our parents, not the abuse. We honor the person who has been given the position, not the evil, degrading acts. Not their wrong choices. Not their damaging, wounding acts against us.

Use extreme caution as you seek to build a relationship with abusive parents. If your case is severe—such as habitual sexual abuse or extreme emotional trauma—it may be wise for you to avoid personal contact. You also may need to protect your children. And in cases like these, it's important to seek counsel from those who are experienced in knowing how such protection can work.

If You Want to Write a Tribute

I've written a great deal in this book about honoring your parents with a written tribute. This may not be possible for you; maybe you just can't bring yourself to write a tribute and give it to your parents. If so, I'd like to suggest that you go through the process of writing a tribute that will be only for you to read. Use the process of writing the tribute as a way of expressing yourself and your faith to God. You may even want to write a tribute to God, giving thanks for the parents He gave you. Perhaps the expression of forgiveness, love, and honor that comes through this private tribute will promote healing in your soul . . . and bring you one step closer to actually being able to present the tribute to your parents.

Use the process of writing the tribute as a way of expressing yourself and your faith to God.

If you do attempt to honor your parents with a written document such as a tribute, here are two suggestions:

First, be patient as you work to reclaim positive memories. Perhaps as you've read this book you've traversed the landscape of your mind in search of good memories with your parents, only to find a parched, barren wilderness. You may have searched your soul to gather enough pleasant memories to fill a tribute—but you've come up empty.

Good memories are like roses—fragrant and alive, vivid and lingering in our minds. You may go in search of a field of roses, only to find you couldn't gather enough to fill a vase. If this is so, then admit your disappointment and anger. And ask God to show you where they are growing.

You may have to acknowledge the possibility that your parents may have planted some roses but you can't remember them. Those roses may be surrounded by a thicket of thorn bushes that need to be uprooted to reveal the flowers.

Finally, keep your expectations in check. Go with an obedient heart, but beware of expecting a positive response. If your parents do respond positively to your tribute, then healing can begin. But if they don't, ask God to enable you to fulfill the command of Romans 12:18: "If possible, so far as it depends on you, live peaceably with all."

(16)

HELPING OTHERS HONOR THEIR PARENTS

Nobody's family can hang out the sign "Nothing the matter here."

—Chinese proverb

I was teaching a Sunday school class of about sixty-five sixth graders about the importance of loving someone who seems unlovable. For many of those preteens, that may have been a pesky little brother or sister, or a cruel classmate at school.

Nina Cameron, a friend and one of the parents assisting, shared a story that hit me and the class like an emotional freight train. I'd like to share the story here in Nina's own words because it demonstrates how one person can help another give honor to a needy parent.

Nina embodies how Christ's love can penetrate the surface of even the crustiest individual. Some parents may not look worthy of honor, but peel away the facade and you may find a tender heart—and, in this case, a parent waiting to be loved.

My daughter, Natalie, and I visited a nursing home for several years, and there was one particular lady there who was so offensive and grumpy that no one wanted anything to do with her. But somehow the Lord gave me a real burden and love for Mary. I began to try to reach out and be her friend.

Unfortunately, the harder I tried, the more distant Mary became. When we came in to visit her, she would make some crude remark and turn her back to us.

Determined not to be discouraged, we continued trying to find a spark of interest that would reveal a way to show love for her. One day I asked Mary, "Isn't there anything you like?"

She looked at me out of the corner of her eyes and mumbled, "I like butterscotch candy, and I like to draw." I asked what she liked to draw and she replied, "See for yourself. There's a box under my bed."

We pulled out the dirty box and inside were sheets of notebook paper with some of the most beautiful sketches of flowers and women's designs I had ever seen. Looking through them, I caught a glimpse of the woman she once had been—a talented artist who could take a simple sunflower or bluebird and turn it into a masterpiece.

When I praised her ability to draw, Mary looked at Natalie, who was about five, and said, "Well, if you could get her to sit still, I'd draw her picture." Natalie agreed and jumped up on her bed. As I watched Mary draw, I could see a talented artist at work, taking note of every detail of my daughter's features. A part of her seemed to come alive, and for a moment she forgot where she was.

During our subsequent visits, we tried to coax her to draw again, but usually she wanted nothing to do with us. She still didn't like anything about us, right down to my name, Nina. She decided to call me Luke instead.

Her eyes were getting so bad that she could not read very well. So one day I asked if she would like me to bring a Bible and read to her. "Luke, I don't like that religious stuff," she replied, "and I don't want to hear anything about it again."

It seemed that she rejected every word and every attempt of kindness we offered her. But I could tell she was warming up to us, even though she would never admit it.

Several months of these visits went by and then she developed cancer. She was in the hospital for quite a while, and when she returned to the nursing home, I realized she would not live much longer. I asked her to tell me about her family and she told me she had a son in New York whom she had not seen in six years.

As I left the nursing home that day I felt a heaviness of heart that is hard to explain. It was as if Jesus Himself was in the car with me. When I arrived home, I dialed information for New York and got the son's phone number. I called him, introduced myself, and told him I had been visiting his mother in the nursing home.

There was dead silence—I could almost feel the coldness. I asked God to penetrate through his pain, and at that moment he began to weep. "Lady, I don't know who you are, but I love my mother," he said.

I asked if he would consider coming out to see her before she died. He said he wanted to, but he didn't have the money. When I hung up the phone, I could tell by the way my heart was aching that it could not end this way. My husband and I decided to pay for the son's plane ticket, plus a hotel room when he arrived in Little Rock.

I called the son back and told him what we were going to do. "Why are you doing this, lady?" he asked.

"Because I'm a Christian and in the Bible Jesus told us that when we have helped the least of these, 'you did it to Me,' " I explained.

A few days later I picked up the son at the airport and drove him to the nursing home. I was not sure what the reunion would be like after all these years and all the pain that had kept them apart. But when he walked into his mother's room, she called his name and they fell into each other's arms, weeping. I quietly left the room, but I was not alone. The look on Mary's face and the joy in her eyes went with me.

While the son was in Little Rock, I was able to tell him about Christ and my life with Him. I also brought him to church on Sunday. He said he could not remember how long it had been since he had been in a church.

As it happened, our pastor spoke about the blood of Christ in the sermon that morning. Afterward the son said he wanted to tell his mother what he had heard.

He spent the next several days sitting by her bedside, talking to her and rubbing lotion onto her dry, wrinkled skin. He bought her a scarf that she wore on her bald head. He drew pictures for her that she had taught him to draw many years before, when he was a little boy.

When I took the son to the airport at the end of his visit, he told me, "There are not words in the English language to express how I feel." And when I returned to the nursing home, for the first time I saw a glow of peace on Mary's face. She looked at me, took my hand, and said, "Luke, I love you."

I knew it was the first time in many, many years she had felt love, or at least had let her guard down enough to say it. The next thing she said was, "I want you to bring that Bible and read it to me when you come back."

She died before I had a chance to visit again, but she died with peace in her heart and with her unfinished business resolved. She died knowing that God loved her.

Encouraging Others to Do What's Right

As you have seen by the stories I have told in this book, some special blessings are reserved for those who obey God's commandment to honor their parents. Nina's experience reveals another type of blessing—the joy of helping others honor their parents.

It may be your spouse, a friend, family members, perhaps even brothers or sisters who need to honor their parents just as much as you do. All they may need is your prompting and encouragement to help them execute what could be one of the most important things they'll ever do in their lives.

It is possible your siblings will resent you for suggesting they honor your parents. Explain the reason for honoring your parents, but let them know you have no desire to pressure them.

Hebrews 10:24 encourages us to "consider how to stir up one another to love and good works." In some cases, this may be as simple as involving your brothers and sisters in your tribute.

This especially works well for major celebrations such as a wedding anniversary. Let them know in a phone call or letter that you have had a growing conviction of your responsibility to honor your parents. If appropriate, let them know there may be shortcomings in your parents for which you could reject them, but you feel compelled to honor them for the things they did right. Tell them about the process you have gone through to come to this point, and ask them to write a tribute, too.

If you come from a difficult family, it is possible your siblings will resent you for even suggesting they honor your parents. If you face a situation like this, clearly explain the reason for honoring your parents, but let them know you have no desire to place any pressure on them. You may be able to encourage them gently to deal with their bitterness and anger, because it will be better for them in the long run. You may also need to help them understand how they have been hurt, and then show them how to move beyond that pain to compassion and forgiveness.

Are You Helping or Hindering Your Spouse?

After marriage, it's common for us to see our parents in a different light. Each of us comes from a separate family history, and we relate to our parents in a certain way. Then a new person comes into the family, and the dynamics change. Your spouse brings a new perspective to the situation, observing your parents' strengths and faults and noting how they affect you. At this point, you and your spouse have some choices to make. Will you be a positive or a negative influence for each other in this area?

Jessica's father was a successful lawyer, a powerful man who was accustomed to getting his own way. He had provided for his family quite well financially, but he had been so preoccupied with building a career that he had largely neglected his family. He was opinionated, blunt, and bossy. When they failed to meet his standards, he belittled his children with cruel and sarcastic remarks.

Jessica sometimes wished her father was different, but over the years she grew accustomed to him and his ways. That began to change, however, when she married Ryan. A young insurance salesman, he was quite driven himself. So it was inevitable that he would feel some tension with his new father-in-law. Out of respect—and perhaps a little fear—Ryan acted politely during the first few times he spent with Jessica's father. Even if the man said something he completely disagreed with, Ryan held his tongue. Alone with Jessica, however, he expressed his frustration.

"How can you take that man?" he asked one night as they drove home following a family dinner. "He treats you like a little kid, he always has to be in control, and he thinks he's right about everything!"

"He's my dad," Jessica replied. "I know he's got his faults, but that doesn't mean I shouldn't love him."

By the time they reached home, Jessica was depressed. Memories she had suppressed for many years—of birthday parties missed, of hugs she wanted from her dad but never received—came flooding back.

Over the next few years, this pattern continued. To avoid any conflict, Ryan mainly kept to himself when they visited Jessica's family. But he heard everything that went on and led a debriefing session while driving home. Jessica, meanwhile, found herself feeling more resentment and anger toward her father. She wondered why God could not have put her in a different family, with a father who loved her.

Ryan and Jessica found themselves feeling increasingly alienated from her parents. On one hand this was easier, because the less time they spent with them, the less tension, pressure, and anger they felt. But deep inside, Jessica wished it was different. When a friend mentioned her father, she would say, "I wish I could find a way to break through to my father, but he's so cold."

What Ryan did not realize was that he was the main problem. By dissecting each family visit during the drive home, he pushed his wife to focus on her father's negative attributes. He brought confusion and tension into her life because he was encouraging her to alienate herself from a man who, despite his faults, she loved deeply.

Ryan needed to help his wife honor her dad.

Where's Your Focus?

Tensions with parents and in-laws are inevitable in a marriage. But a married couple needs to make a mutual commitment early in their relationship to avoid focusing on the negative. Encourage each other to give parents a lot of grace, to overlook offenses, and to be lavish with forgiveness. Talk about the things parents are doing right.

As difficult as this may sound, another thought should be even more sobering: Do you really want to be the one preventing your spouse from obeying one of God's commandments?

(17)

ARE YOU WORTHY OF HONOR?

A good character is the best tombstone. Those who loved you and were helped by you, will remember you. So carve your name on hearts and not on marble.

—C. H. Spurgeon

Years ago I had an unusual speaking opportunity. First I addressed a group of teenagers, exhorting them to heed the command of Ephesians 6:1–3, which instructs children to obey and honor their parents. Then I had the opportunity to speak about the same passage to the parents of those teens. But the moment I'll never forget from that gathering was when Dr. Henry Brandt, a psychiatrist from West Palm Beach, Florida, posed this question to those parents: "Are you worthy of honor?"

I remember the room was strangely quiet. Most had never considered the question. And many had to answer Brandt with a sheepish, "No . . . I'm really not worthy."

Throughout this book, I have exhorted you as a child to honor your parents. I've encouraged you to honor them for what they did right, not blame them for what they did wrong. God expects us to honor our parents regardless of their practice.

Consider the flipside of the forgotten commandment: how can you make it as easy as possible for your children to honor you?

Now, I'd like you to consider the flipside of the forgotten commandment: how can you make it as easy as possible for your children to honor *you*?

It's been fascinating to read through copies of the tributes people have written over the years. The memories in these tributes formed a mosaic of what a family ought to be. Over and over, these children considered three things important:

- Their parent's involvement
- Their parent's emotional support
- Their parent's character

Let's consider how we can become a parent worthy of honor by building these qualities into our lives.

Principle #1: Your children will remember your involvement.

Your children need more than your time; they need your attention. They flourish when you focus on them.

This means more than just showing up at soccer games. Children need your heart knitted to theirs as they make choices and hammer out their character. They need you to know what's going on in their lives. They need you to help them think about the clothing they wear, the type of person they date, and the peer pressure they face.

In order to be a parent worthy of honor you can't just *be* there, you have to be *all* there.

That sounds simple, but it's easy to fill your hours away from work with television shows, the Internet, hobbies, finances, books, shopping, and housework. If you were able to add up how much time you actually spend focusing on your children each week, you might be shocked to discover that your total would be measured in minutes, not hours.

Being all there does not mean you do it perfectly every time, but it does mean that you are keeping the lines of communication firmly open and intact.

A couple of the tributes I received serve as penetrating reminders:

> Dad, I can still remember afternoons in our backyard pitching baseball, passing the football, shooting hoops, or doing whatever sport the season called for. . . .

> Thank you for all the wonderful childhood memories: of playing in the sprinkler after a hard day's work in the yard; of going to Playland Amusement Park and riding the roller coaster and shooting darts; of all the wonderful camping trips and water skiing until we dropped; of riding around at Christmas looking at all the pretty lights. Thank you for all the delicious barbecue, and of course the memories would not be complete without remembering how we listened to Kentucky Wildcat basketball games on the radio!

I've noticed that adult children usually don't highlight grand vacations in their lists of favorite memories. Instead they've remembered the simpler times of playing games, playing ball, fishing, and camping.

Also, I've found it interesting that these tributes rarely mention television, as in, "Thanks for all those times we watched TV together." It's *personal* interaction that kids remember.

After a couple attended a Weekend to Remember marriage getaway, the husband immediately walked into the family room and unplugged the TV. With the cord dangling and wide-eyed kids in tow, he lugged the set to the garage. In the empty place where the television once stood, he hung a picture of the family. Their five-year-old son sat down on the floor, staring at the portrait. Then he looked up at his dad and asked, "Does this mean we're going to become a family now?"

Principle #2: Your children will remember your emotional support.

I will never forget a counseling appointment many years ago. A mom sat in my office and told the story of her eleven-year-old son's relationship with his dad. The father, a hard-driving and successful businessman, constantly criticized the boy.

"You dummy, you left the door open!"

"Look at these grades! That's pitiful!"

"You struck out at the game! I can't believe you did that!"

"Look at your room! It's a mess and so are you!"

By my estimate that boy is in his late forties now. And I'll bet he still hears an inner recording repeatedly playing, "You're a failure! You can't do it! Why try?"

Some of you who read this know exactly what I am talking about.

You know how painful it feels to hear that inner recording, day after day. Is this the type of recording you want for your children?

Reading through tributes, I've also observed how often adults remembered the positive emotional support they received from their parents.

> I can't remember a time that you didn't accept me. I was always OK. My performance was OK, too, as long as I tried my hardest.

> You encouraged me to develop the musical talents God had given me. You told me about how it thrilled you to feel me stir within you before I was even born whenever music was being played at church. . . . You were always there to encourage me in my piano lessons and shine with pride at my success. Those seeds grew in me to where today I can't imagine not being part of my church choir or not having music in my home.

How often do you tell your children you love them, or forgive them? Your kids should hear these words so often that they have no idea how often you've said them.

Another way to give your children emotional support is by utilizing the power of the printed word. Letters and notes are tangible reminders to your children that you love and care for them. Young children, especially, will treasure your handwritten notes of affection.

By filling and refilling our child's emotional tank, you and I become worthy of honor.

Emotional support is also felt when we physically touch our children. Hugs, tight embraces, and kisses are all the steady practice of a parent who wishes to be worthy of honor.

When our kids were little I used to ask them what kind of a bear hug they wanted: a baby bear hug, a mama bear hug, or a papa bear hug. Each hug increased in intensity and a growl. They usually started out with a baby bear hug and worked their way up to the papa bear hug, where I'd nearly squeeze the breath out of them.

I've found that if dads give physical and emotional affection when their children are young, it won't be nearly as difficult when they become teens. It's difficult sometimes to hug teenagers because they act like they don't need it. But that's just a facade.

I'll never forget Barbara hugging our son Benjamin after a rough day at his junior high. She let go; he didn't. He was admitting, nonverbally, "I may be nearly as tall as you, and I may look grown up, and I may act like I don't need affection, but I do!"

By filling and refilling our child's emotional tank, you and I become worthy of honor.

Principle #3: Your children will remember your character.

Someone has said, "Our children are messengers we send to a time we shall not see." As a parent, what kind of message are you sending to the next generation? Is your message and your life worthy of being emulated and honored?

As a parent, you have the incredible responsibility of shaping the moral conscience of the next generation. Even though your children will grow up to make their own choices, the character qualities you model and teach will help mold them and give them direction. In fact, I've noticed that many children, after passing through years of rebellion against their parents, settle into adulthood by adopting many of the same character qualities that they once railed against.

Once again, I found these character qualities highlighted often in the tributes I've read.

> You taught me through example to honor and respect my elders, to establish a strong work ethic, and to complete a task with excellence. You are a man of your word.

> Mom, you are a woman of strength and devotion. Your determination is a beautiful gift from the Lord. Your perseverance, tolerance, patience, honesty, integrity, and ethics are not to be surpassed. Words like *kind, thoughtful, caring,* and *gentle* were created to describe you. You are loving, giving, compassionate, and generous.

> Mom showed me what it was to have faith in God. She taught me how to love God and worship Him and serve Him. Mom showed me what generosity and sacrificial giving was all about.

What character qualities do you want to pass on to your children? What do you believe in? What are your core values?

The Roman philosopher Seneca said, "You must know for which harbor you are headed if you are to catch the right wind to take you there." If you've determined what your core values are, then you can find creative ways to teach and model them to your children.

A Special Challenge to Dads

Over the last few decades, too many fathers have pulled back from leadership in their families. To a large degree, we who call ourselves "dads" are responsible for this paralysis of character in our homes. Too many of us are passively disengaged, consumed with our careers, preoccupied with our toys and hobbies. Too disengaged to get involved with our kids' lives.

Real men with real character act; they take responsibility head on. They may not do it perfectly, but they tackle issues courageously. They are men worthy of honor. They step up when faced with tough challenges.*

Men, we need to hear and heed Paul's words to the church at Corinth: "Be watchful, stand firm in the faith, act like men, be strong. Let all that you do be done in love" (1 Corinthians 16:13–14).

We've got to encourage one another to be involved and not abandon our kids to the culture. We've got to do it because God is going to hold us responsible for how we protect our families.

---

* If you are in need of stepping up, check out my book, *Stepping Up: A Call to Courageous Manhood.* In it, I equip men to step up and move through five phases that every man was designed to fulfill.

Men, your hearts need to be connected to the hearts of your children. You may need to cry out in prayer to the divine surgeon who specializes in that type of surgery. The last verse of the Old Testament, Malachi 4:6, gives us His promise: "And he will turn the hearts of fathers to their children and the hearts of children to their fathers, lest I come and strike the land with a decree of utter destruction."

God will help you be worthy of honor and involved in your child's life. Just ask Him to reconnect your heart to your children's.

A Night of Surprises

Satchel Paige, a baseball hall of famer and occasional philosopher, once said, "What goes around, comes around."

Barbara and I saw how true those words are at the end of the summer of 1992. During a FamilyLife staff banquet, we were brought up front for a question-and-answer session. But to our surprise, the master of ceremonies announced that the real purpose of the entire evening was to honor us for our upcoming twentieth wedding anniversary.

Several good friends who had been hiding in the back of the room were brought up to say a few words. But the real highlight came when all six of our children showed up. Little Laura, seven at the time, went first, standing on a chair. She had written a tribute with the help of her sister and brothers: "Thank you, Mom, for all the dresses you made me. For hugs and kisses. For being a great Mom. Dad, thanks for being my ice cream buddy, for the stories you tell at bedtime, and for wrestling with me."

One down, five to go. I looked at Barbara and both of us were choking back the tears.

Deborah, the next to youngest at age nine, was the next to stand on the chair and speak. In her quiet, soft voice she thanked her mom for helping her with homework and cutting her hair short. She thanked me for taking her on fishing dates and out to eat. Then she turned to both of us, looking us in the eyes with a big grin on her face, and said, "And I want to thank both of you for adopting me when I was a baby."

That did it! Barbara and I were basket cases. Tears were streaming down our faces. We boo-hooed through the four other children.

The evening will go down as one of the greatest privileges we've ever experienced. After all those years of showing children how to honor their parents, we had the opportunity to experience what it was like, as parents, to receive that honor. It felt great. We had experienced the promise of Ephesians 6:3—"that it may go well with you"—in that we had honored our parents and now we were being honored by our children.

There is much about the command and promise of Exodus 20:12 that I still have yet to apply and understand. It would be my prayer that you would get in the process of fulfilling your responsibility to your parents and experience the privileges of obedience.

I pray that you will do what's right and seek to obey God by honoring your parents, and that you will experience God's abundant blessings and favor as a result of your obedience.

APPENDIX

QUESTIONS TO HELP YOU UNLOCK YOUR MEMORIES

As you put together a tribute, the following list will help you capture special memories from your childhood. Not all these questions will apply to you, but quite a few will.

Favorite Memories

What's your first memory of your mom? Your dad?

What school projects did they help you with?

What was your favorite gift your dad or mom ever got you?

What memorable conversations do you recall having with your parents?

Where did you go on vacations? What did you do?

What was your favorite vacation?

What was your happiest moment as a child?

What did you enjoy doing with your dad?

What did you enjoy doing with your mom?

What was your favorite moment with your dad?

What was your favorite moment with your mom?

What smells remind you of your dad? Your mom?

What sounds accompanied your home life growing up?

Where was the warmest spot (not physically but emotionally) in your house?

What was your favorite room in your house?

What was the first movie you ever remember seeing?

What TV shows did you watch regularly as a family?

What was your favorite book your parents read to you?

What songs did you sing together?

What was your favorite restaurant to go to?

Who was your favorite relative to visit as a family?

What do you remember about your dad's or mom's workplace?

What hobbies did your parents enjoy?

What holiday traditions did you observe?

What were weekends like at your house?

What was your favorite tradition?

Did you ever climb in bed with your parents?

If you woke up scared from a nightmare, what did you do? How did your mom or dad respond to you?

What problems did they help you with as a child? As a teenager?

What pets did they get for you?

What "dates" did you go on together?

What activities did they encourage you to be involved in?

What activities did they participate in with you (as a coach, teacher, etc.)?

What are your favorite family games? Game with Dad? Mom?

Family Funnies

What were the family jokes?

What was the funniest moment you experienced with your dad? Your mom? Your family when everyone was there?

What special phrases did your family invent?

What nicknames did people in your family have, and how did they earn them?

Holidays and Celebrations

What costumes did you wear on Halloween? Where did you get them?

What was your favorite Christmas present?

What was your favorite birthday?

Character Qualities

What did other people think of your parents? How did they react to them? How did they treat your father or mother at work?

What did you admire about your parents?

How did your parents display affection for you?

How did your parents display affection for each other?

What's one thing you appreciate that your dad often did for your mother? Or vice versa?

How did they treat other people?

Do you remember seeing your parents cry?

What values that you learned from them are you now passing on to your children?

What character qualities did they model that have stuck with you?

What sacrifices did they make for you?

Their Legacy

What character qualities do you owe to your dad? Your mom?

What hobbies, skills, or interests did they pass on to you?

What else did they teach you how to do?

What did you learn from your parents about work?

What did they teach you about life?

What values did they pass on to you?

What advice did they give you that you are grateful for?

What was the greatest lesson you ever learned from your mom? From your dad?

What did they teach you about being a parent?

In what ways are you like them in your personality, skills, habits, etc.?

What character qualities did they model as a couple that have stuck with you?

NOTES

Chapter 1

1. Bobbie Gee, “Quality of Life,” *Buy-Line,* Winter 1991, 5.

Chapter 4

1. John MacArthur, *Ephesians* (Chicago: Moody Press, 1986), 312–315.
2. Alan Loy McGinnis, *The Friendship Factor* (Minneapolis: Augsburg Publishing, 1979), 30.

Chapter 8

1. J. Wesley Brown, “Good News for Parents,” *Christian Century* (May 1, 1981), 513.
2. Phyllis McCormack, "Look Closer." LenClark.com. http://www.lenclark.com/Look%20Closer.htm (24 March 2004). Reprinted with permission by Michael E. McCormack.

Chapter 9

1. Ivan Maisel, “Derek Redman,” *Dallas Morning News* (August 4, 1992), 17B.

Chapter 10

1. Elaine L. Schulte, “The Day Before My Father Died,” *Decision,* (June 1981), 27.
2. Lewis B. Smedes, “Forgiveness: The Power to Change the Past,” *Christianity Today* (January 7, 1983): 22.
3. Smedes, “Forgiveness” 22.

Chapter 11

1. Ney Bailey, *Faith Is Not a Feeling* (Nashville: Thomas Nelson Publishers, 1978), 42, 45–46.

Chapter 14

1. Paul Tsongas, "Happy to Be Here," *People,* (May 3, 1993), 179.

Chapter 15

1. Dan Allender, *The Wounded Heart: Hope for Adult Victims of Childhood Sexual Abuse* (Colorado Springs: NavPress, 1990), 179.
2. Allender, *The Wounded Heart,* 238.
3. Allender, *The Wounded Heart,* 184.